THE AMERICAN
CUSTOM
CAR

PAT GANAHL

MBI Publishing Company

DEDICATION

To Sam Barris, Gil and Al Ayala, Harry Westergard, Joe Wilhelm, Bill Cushenbery, and so many other pioneering customizers who were devil with a hammer and hell with a torch, but who are no longer with us, this book is dedicated. To the many other great customizers who are still cutting, welding, and teaching—you'll have to wait your turn.

First published in 2001 by MBI Publishing Company, Galtier Plaza, Suite 200, 380 Jackson Street, St. Paul, MN 55101-3885, USA.

© Pat Ganahl, 2001

MBI Publishing Company books are also available at discounts in bulk quantity for industrial or sales-promotional use. For details write to Special Sales Manager at Motorbooks International Wholesalers & Distributors, Galtier Plaza, Suite 200, 380 Jackson Street, St. Paul, MN 55101-3885, USA.

Library of Congress Cataloging-in-Publication Data Available
ISBN: 0-7603-0950-7

On the cover: The legendary Hirohata Merc represents an obvious turning point in customizing, when builders began to think more was better. It was the first '51 to be chopped by George and Sam Barris, the first to use Buick side chrome—plus so much more. It all works beautifully on this car. *Steve Coonan*

On the frontis: Lee Pratt's purple '41 Buick fastback gleams in the sunlight.

On the title page: Ray Kress' lime-gold '56 Mercury is an excellent example of the later 1950s semi custom style.

On the endpapers: The Satan's Angels of Hayward was the Bay Area custom car club of the 1950s.

Edited by: Steve Hendrickson
Designed by: Katie Sonmor

Printed in China

CONTENTS

PREFACE

I WANT TO BEGIN

by thanking my long-time friend and colleague Steve Hendrickson, who, shortly after arriving at MBI Publishing as acquisitions editor, called and asked me if I would like to do this book. It wasn't my idea, it was his. But I think it was an excellent idea.

The plan for this work was to be more or less a companion piece to Dean Batchelor's *The American Hot Rod*, which is really the only book that describes, defines, and delineates hot rodding in general as a history and as a culture. I had planned to do such a book myself, but he beat me to it. More power to him, and he was the perfect writer to do it. Rest his soul.

Similarly, until now, there had never been any sort of book covering the history of the custom car in America. Even books on specific aspects of customizing have been scarce until recently. Thanks to Andy Southard Jr., George Barris, and one or two others, we are finally getting a look at some excellent photo archive material that has lain dormant for too long. But nobody had ever attempted to compile a historical overview that puts this American automotive cultural phenomenon into perspective. It was my pleasure to do so, and I must tell you it was an amazing learning experience—as any worthwhile book project should be. I thought I knew this subject. Little did I know.

Since this is the preface to the work, there is one thing I must bring up. There are an awful lot of *people* left out, who were (or are) central to the history of customizing—be they builders, car owners, show promoters, magazine writers/photographers—who are not present in this text, or may be only obliquely mentioned. This is not to overlook or snub anyone. It is a matter of space and time. There is room for another book on "The Customizers." But here I wanted to concentrate more on the cars themselves: how they began, how they evolved, how they got sidetracked, how they got put back on track, how they continue to evolve today. This is, I think, plenty enough for one book.

Speaking of people, there are a few I must thank for their help getting this book built. First and foremost is NHRA Historian Greg Sharp, who could have easily written this book better than I. Whether it's custom cars, hot rods, drag racing, or any other offshoot of the genre, he has it in his head. And he probably also has it in his photo files and library. For years I have pestered Greg with my "20 questions" phone calls, and he only gets mad at me every once in a long while. We have swapped photos back and forth between our collections for years, and I usually come out on the better end of the deal. Thanks Greg, you've been especially helpful on this project.

Likewise, George Barris has been immensely gracious with his huge photo collection, his personal stories, and his reminiscences of points in the custom car history.

Thanks to the many players who let me stick a tape recorder in their face and take up their time, either specifically for this book or in the past: Joe Bailon, Dick Bertolucci, Neil Emory, Bill Hines, Dick Dean, Larry Watson, George Bistagne, Tom Sparks, Junior Conway, Dean Jeffries, Lee Pratt, Spence Murray . . . I should have done lots more.

And to the many who contributed personal photos, magazine articles, books, and so on, beginning with Kurt McCormick, whose "stuff" is incredible, and who almost lost a significant portion of it to a U.S. Mail mishap (they redeemed themselves). Also in this group are *Custom Rodder* Editor Jerry Weesner, Jack Walker, Doug Reed, Darrel Arment, Keith Ashley, the late Dean Batchelor, Gary Minor, and probably several more that my now near-dead brain is refusing to remember.

And finally, of course, to my wife, Anna, whose typical comment as I raced through this project was, "You wrote what today? No!" Honestly, she has always been my worst (best) critic and staunchest supporter. Thanks for all the "Atta Boys," sweetheart. Sometimes they come when they're most needed.

INTRODUCTION

This gorgeous vehicle was built by George Du Vall and Frank Kurtis for the Southern California Plating Co. in 1936 to work as a delivery truck by day and a midget pull-start car on weekend evenings. It sports a handmade grille, the prototype Du Vall V-windshield, and a custom Carson top. Both Du Vall and Kurtis customized numerous vehicles, but none fit the guidelines of the American custom car as delineated in this book. Let the arguments fly.

WHAT IS A CUSTOM CAR?

WE IN THE HOT ROD

fraternity tend to take rods and customs for granted. We know what their salient characteristics are, and we know what distinguishes the two. Although hot rods and custom cars are closely related, they are two very different types of vehicles.

The general public seems to have a pretty good grasp of what a hot rod is, but seems somewhat confused about what constitutes a custom. Indeed, several of the builders of these cars, both today and yesterday, also seem a bit confused about what elements should be included in a well-proportioned, flowing custom car design.

To say that any custom-bodied car—whether modified from a production vehicle, totally reskinned by a coachbuilder, or constructed from the ground up—is a "custom" as discussed in this book is incorrect. The customs we are concerned with derived from hot rod culture in the 1940s and 1950s, nearly disappeared in the 1960s and early 1970s, then reemerged in the late 1970s and continue to develop today.

The earliest hot rods (called gow jobs or hop ups at the time) evolved in Southern California in the late 1920s and Depression-era 1930s, and were mostly Model T and A roadsters that were stripped down to bare bones for lightness and streamlining, then hopped up with racing engine parts left over from the heady circle track racing craze of the 'teens and early 1920s. Most of these early "rodders" were teenagers or guys in their early 20s. They had very little money, and the emphasis was on racing, whether on the street or on the high desert dry lakes (usually both).

But this was also a social activity. They formed clubs with names like Road Runners, Low Flyers, Vultures, Bungholers, and Albata. They had plaques on their cars and wore jackets or jumpsuits with the name and emblem on the back to proclaim their club loyalty. The various clubs held their meetings and generally hung out at their favored drive-in, restaurant, or gas station. They had their own clothing styles. They spoke their own slang. It was a culture.

The gow jobs were certainly fast. But they were rudimentary, they were often temperamental and unreliable, they offered no shelter from the elements, and they were anything but comfortable. As these roadster jockeys graduated to better-paying jobs and possibly families, a more practical form of transportation became not only affordable, but preferable. They might have kept their low-dollar roadsters for weekend hell-raising or racing, but for driving to work and carrying the wife or kids, they wanted something a little newer, more comfortable, and with windows that would roll up if it rained.

While the roadsters were nearly always stripped of fenders, tops, and hoods, and had big

We generally say customs begin with '35 fat-fender models, but this '34 roadster, with its fender skirts, solid hood, spinner wheelcovers, lowered and elongated headlights, V-windshield, and '40 Lincoln bumpers, is definitely customized, not rodded. It even appears to have smooth, painted running boards.

This is a young, proud Bill Burke with his near-new '36 three-window. While it does have solid hood sides, the other additions—fog lights, fender lights, fender chrome strips, mud flaps, and '34 bumpers—are not what we would call custom touches. This car is "accessorized" rather than customized. Bill was also a pioneer dry lakes racer (he built the first belly tank lakester), and later worked in the automotive magazine business.

What is this? It appears to be a '38 Buick convertible that someone shortened into a single seater, with a reworked front end and full fadeaway fenders. Supposedly built before the war in the Pasadena area, it could have been modified by Bohman and Schwartz—or by most any local body shop. It has custom touches like the skirts, spinners, and chopped top, but it doesn't fit our definition of custom.

rather than speed. While the hot rods were fast, loud, and arrogant, the customs were slow, classy, and a bit sinister. Hot rods raced; customs cruised. The open-wheeled roadsters, with big tires in the back and little tires in the front, sat on a nose-down "rake." The customs, usually with skirts covering the rear wheels, sat low all around, or even lower in the back than in the front, kind of like a cruising speedboat. And while most rods were topless, the customs, even if they were open cars, usually had cut-down, padded, nonfolding tops that were rarely removed.

While the roadsters were literally streamlined for racing at the dry lakes (where wind resistance is the primary drawback to speed), the customs were streamlined for style. Hence the chopped (lowered) tops, the lowering of the car, the fender skirts, the filled seams, the rounded corners, the lengthened fenders. The lines of a well-proportioned custom would all merge at some vanishing point well behind the vehicle.

It is often said that a rivalry existed between rodders and customizers, but the truth is that most customizers started out with hot roadsters. The custom owners had their own clubs, plaques, and jackets, just like the rodders, and many clubs included both rods and customs. Many participants, even today, own rods and customs concurrently, or in succession. The title of the long-standing magazine, *Rod & Custom*, surely indicates that both belong to the same culture.

However, when hot rodding (a name applied as a pejorative by newspaper journalists) exploded as a teen craze in the years just after World War II, many young new rodders couldn't understand why anyone would spend money on modifications that didn't improve a

Here are two different, though similar, versions of "customs" seen at an early Indianapolis car show. The sports-car-like cut-down doors were a Midwest trend, seen on both street and track roadsters. They're highly customized. Call them custom cars if you want. I'd say the one with the Lincoln grille, sideways '40 headlights, and big bird on the hood has been "uglified."

tires in the back for higher gearing at the dry lakes and better traction on the street, the newer (1935 and later) "fat-fender" cars just didn't look good with the fenders off. But since the owners of these newer cars had grown up in the hot rod culture, they couldn't leave these cars alone. They had to fix 'em up, alter them, modify them, personalize them.

So a new style developed, catering more to the newer cars, and the emphasis was on style,

car's performance. Many customizers, on the other hand, were content to keep their smoothed and lacquered hoods shut and their drivetrains stock. Further, the lead used to fill and recontour these large, heavy-to-begin-with cars added considerably to their weight (plastic fillers, such as Bondo, weren't invented until the 1960s), making them that much slower on the street. Some hot rodders derided them as "leadsleds."

Part of the so-called rivalry no doubt stemmed from jealousy. You had to have some bucks to build a custom, since they were made from nearly new cars. The body modifications required considerably more expertise (and tools) than stripping down a rod and hopping up its engine, so the work was usually farmed out to professional custom or body shops. The same went for the lush lacquer paint jobs and lavish tuck-and-roll interiors. And once this cool custom was completed, you can imagine the impression it made on the young ladies at the drive-in on Friday night. That was part of the plan.

Yet despite being expensive compared to rods, the customs still had that make-it-better, do-it-yourself rebel demeanor. They were built primarily from lower-priced cars such as Fords, Chevys, and Mercurys, but most of the customizing—lowering, lengthening, stretching the front fenders to the rear—gave them the look of more expensive cars like Buicks and Cadillacs. Customizers often incorporated parts from these cars, such as Cadillac grilles and wheel covers, Buick side chrome and fender skirts, and Packard or Lincoln taillights. And while the removal of name badges and other excess chrome cleaned up the lines of the custom, it further disguised the car's identity. Part of the reason for customizing was to

lend mystery to the car, to baffle the unknowing, even, as mentioned, to give the car a sinister edge.

As we shall see, the traditional custom era, highlighted by chopped '39–'51 Mercs, '36–'51 Fords, and '40–'54 Chevys, really lasted only about a decade, before they were upstaged by the longer, lower, finned hardtops from Detroit in the latter 1950s, and then by the musclecars of the 1960s. During the dormant period that followed, customizing morphed in several directions, some rather misguided and egged on by car show promoters and magazine covers. But given hot rodding's rebirth as "street rodding" in the early 1970s, I guess it was only natural that traditional customs made a comeback in the later 1970s and 1980s.

Now, as in their heyday, the custom contingent numbers only a fraction (about a third, at most) of the hot rod crowd, possibly for the same initial reasons: higher cost and complicated construction. And while some newer, more contemporary styles are finally emerging, as we shall see in Chapter 10, this crowd (for reasons I don't fully understand) remains very nostalgia-oriented, sticking to the 1940s-1950s styles and working (by definition of the Kustom Kemps of America association) exclusively on 1936–1964 cars. I'd personally love to see some of the newer cars Lincolns, Thunderbirds, maybe some of the Tom Gale–inspired Chrysler products—join the current custom fold (as in the custom's heyday), but this does not seem to be in the cards presently.

Whatever happens, I'm extremely glad the custom car is once again with us, including numerous well-known beauties either replicated or found and restored to their former glory. The smooth shapes, graceful curves, and candy colors of these cool cruisers are a sensual delight.

Johnny Zaro's and Al Andril's chopped '40 Mercs were two standard-issue chopped customs that were built by the Barrises in the late 1940s. Andril's blue car was later owned by surf pioneer Dale Velzy in the early 1950s. Zaro's maroon car has been restored by Kurt McCormick.

GENESIS

EVER SINCE THE BIRTH

of the automobile around the beginning of the last century, owners and others for hire have been modifying or "personalizing" cars in any number of ways, be it tying a raccoon tail to the windshield, adding a windshield, or bolting on a rearview mirror (or "cop spotter"). Owners of Model Ts had as many as a dozen, if not more, companies offering aftermarket bodies to turn their Tin Lizzies into "speedsters," mimicking race cars of the time or sporty models like Stutz Bearcats or Mercer Raceabouts. Even the fledgling *Ford Times* magazine talked more about modifying Model Ts than anything else.

Then we had the coachbuilders, or *carrozzeria* as they were known in Italy. Ranging from design houses to builders of utilitarian vehicles like depot hacks (station wagons) or ambulances, these companies would add custom bodies to factory built running chassis. There were several in Europe that would craft one-off custom bodies for stately Bugattis or Rolls-Royces. In the United States, we had coachbuilders such as Brewster in New York and the Earl Automobile Works, Bohman and Schwartz, Darrin, and Coachcraft in Southern California. These companies usually hand-crafted custom bodies to existing chassis, sometimes using a factory cowl, and in rarer cases they might modify an existing factory body to a new look.

But these are not the American custom cars we are discussing in this book. Coachbuilders created unique high-end cars for the rich. The custom cars we're talking about derived from the decidedly low-end hot rod movement that began in the Depression. True, the customs were a step up from gow jobs, economically, but only a step. In the 25-plus years I've been writing about rods and customs, and interviewing people about this pursuit, I have never found anyone who could say exactly when, where, or how the custom car culture developed. But it was definitely an outgrowth of what was later to be called hot rodding.

The first customs were either owner-built or created in regular body shops to the owner's direction. They were predominantly base-model cars—Fords, Chevys, Mercurys, and maybe a Plymouth or two, modified to look like higher-priced cars, such as Cadillacs, Buicks, Lincolns, or Packards.

Below

We know Link Paola's maroon, chopped, nosed, and decked '40 convert with removed running boards, ripple bumpers, and single-bar flippers was done by September 1939 because he had it finished before the model release date. It's not as low as some, but it fits the pattern, doesn't it?

Right

Let's start with this amazing, grainy photo taken in the Carson Top Shop, because I think this place had a lot to do with the birth—and certainly the proliferation—of the American custom car. The license on that '34 Phaeton on the right might read '41, but the newest of the nine cars pictured is a '39. But besides all the chopped padded tops, look at all the inset license plates, ripple bumpers, and, we assume, teardrop skirts. The style was set by then.

A theme quickly developed among these like-minded customizers that emphasized visual streamlining: lowering; top chopping; removing excess chrome, handles and running boards; and tapering the car from front to rear to make it look more like an airplane.

While some hot rodders disdained the custom owners, or simply couldn't understand why anyone would waste money making a car look fancy if it couldn't go fast, the vast majority of customizers were rodders either before, after, or at the same time. While there were some clubs primarily for custom cars, many clubs included both rods and customs. And while most "lead-sleds" couldn't beat a hopped-up roadster on the street in a drag race, most had engines modified to some extent with the same aftermarket goodies, and many participated at the dry lakes events where they had a better chance of achieving high speed, and where the streamlining actually had a positive effect.

As far as I can determine, these first customs were built shortly after the first "fat-fender" cars came out: '36 Ford three-window coupes and roadsters; '38–'40 Ford convertible sedans, convertibles, and coupes; and early 1940s Chevy convertibles or coupes. As we can see in that amazing, grainy photograph taken at the Carson Top Shop in Los Angeles, the style had certainly been set by the late 1930s. And the Carson Top Shop probably had a lot to do with it.

The point is that a style was set, just as one had been for the hot roadsters. It was a slightly different style, a new one, but these custom owner/builders were from the same fraternity. They might be a little older, and have a little more change in their pockets, but they were still relatively young, they were do-it-yourselfers, they were into cars, and they were taking base models and upgrading them through creative reworking. It was the same ethic as hot rodding and basically the same people, just moving in a slightly different direction with newer cars.

And just like the hot rods, where every car is different, and yet a surprisingly homogenous style is adhered to, the customs very quickly adopted standard dress—with room for creativity. The chassis would be lowered as much as possible (many early customs claimed to be channeled, but weren't). Nearly all wore wide whitewall tires with some sort of full wheelcovers: full moons, Hollywood single bar flippers, and later '49–'50 Cadillac "sombreros." Teardrop skirts for the rear fenders, from a Buick or Packard, were nearly universal. And '37 De Soto "ripple" bumpers were very popular, as were '40 Lincoln Zephyr and '40 Olds bumpers. Recessing the rear license plate and adding a glass cover was very standard, as was removing (or "filling") hood and trunk chrome and emblems and, later, door handles as well.

While there were creative twists here and there, or perhaps regional differences, the overall look of these late 1930s and 1940s customs

Ellis Taylor of Santa Monica nosed and decked this '39 Mercury in 1940, recessed the rear plate, and painted it black in his garage after "some old guy on Pico who did good metalwork" chopped the windshield. The top is a Carson.

was surprisingly similar, like a period style of dress or hairdos. This should be obvious from the accompanying photos. Who built the first custom car in this style? Nobody knows today. I'm pretty sure it developed, most likely in the Los Angeles area, sometime after 1936; given the fact that '37 De Soto bumpers were so popular, it would have to be later than that.

While Amos Carson opened his upholstery shop on South Vermont Avenue in 1927 and advertised "French Tops" in the window, Greg Sharp reported in "The Carson Top Story" in *Hot Rod Yearbook* Number 14 that Carson

A young Neil Emory worked on this slick '37 Dodge convertible in shop class at Burbank high in 1940–1941, recessing both the license and his club plaque and adding '39 Ford taillights to the rear. Burbank Auto Body chopped it and painted it black; Carson did the top. Emory and Clay Jensen, of course, opened Valley Custom later.

Dean Batchelor took this photo of Bill Faris' heavily chopped/Carson topped '38 Ford in front of Neil Emory's house. All were members of the Throttle Stompers club, two of whom graduated from '32 roadsters to customs, demonstrating the hot rod connection.

employee Glen Houser built the first nonfolding, padded, smooth-lined top in 1935 for a '30 Model A Cabriolet. By early 1936, he had constructed a breathtaking, streamlined, chopped padded top for the Southern California Plating "delivery truck" built by George Du Vall and Frank Kurtis from a '35 Ford Phaeton, which also wore the first Du Vall V-windshield. We know the Jarrett Metal Works next door to Carson would chop windshields and side windows to fit the lowered tops, but we don't know if they did other custom work such as dechroming and recessing license plates. But most any good body shop of the time could do this, since they all paddled lead, wielded hammers and dollies, and welded with a torch.

And while there were "custom body" shops in the Los Angeles area dating back to the 1920s, such as Earl and Don Lee Cadillac downtown, Coachcraft on Melrose, and Bohman and Schwartz on Colorado in Pasadena, two of the first to specialize in this new style of moderately customizing base-line production cars in the late 1930s and early 1940s were Jimmy Summers, whose shop was on Melrose near Fairfax, and Roy Hagy, whose best-known shop was on Vermont at Second Street. George Bistagne, who got a slightly used '38 Ford convertible sedan in 1939 or 1940, said he and his older brother Tom went over to Hagy's "Streamline Shop" to learn how to do custom tricks such as chopping the windshield and side windows, filling the hood sides, shaving the nose and deck, recessing the license, and removing the running boards. Bistagne said California Metal Shaping made the rocker panels to replace the running boards, and the rear fender rock shields, which were chromed. With its white Carson top, rich ruby maroon paint, teardrop skirts, De Soto ripple bumpers, single-bar flipper wheelcovers, wide whitewalls, and teardrop taillights, this car completely exemplifies the new custom style we are talking about. After the War, in 1946, the Bistagne Brothers opened their own custom shop in Glendale, performing similar operations on customers' cars, and sending them to Carson for tops, as were several other custom shops around town.

I interviewed Tom Sparks, later of Sparks & Bonney flathead-building fame (among many other things), because he worked for about a year in Hagy's shop around 1942–1943, when he was 15. Tom said he didn't know when Hagy got his start. "It was before my time," he said, noting that

Another couple of young guys learning the custom trade before the war were George Bistagne and his brother Tom, who built this ruby maroon '38 convertible sedan in 1939–1940, with how-to tips from Roy Hagy, running board covers and rock guards from California Metal Shaping, and a Carson top over '34 Cabriolet rear door windows.

Hagy seemed like an old man at the time to him. When Tom was there, Hagy was working in a back room at Russell Johnson's paint shop. "Customs were just starting to come in," said Tom. "Hot rods were '26–'27 T's, '28–'29s, or '32 Fords. But Hagy worked mostly on what we call 'fat-fender' cars today: '36s, '39–'40s. He did mostly filling, removing handles, recessing license plates, and chopping tops. Hagy didn't like to use much lead—he'd metal-finish everything.

"All Hagy did was custom work, but there wasn't much competition. And he always worked alone." Tom said he was just a "sand boy" there, and didn't get paid. But he did learn to gas weld and paint some. Tom pointed out that Hagy built the '40 Ford coupe, which Earle Bruce has owned so many years, for original owner Tommy Winship. Hagy chopped the top, filled the quarter windows, rounded the door corners, and

dechromed it. I asked where this style came from and Tom replied: "I don't know. But they weren't doing it to '33 Plymouths. It had to start sometime in the mid- to late-1930s. They certainly weren't chopping tops on Model Ts."

Tom said that Hagy and Jimmy Summers were the only two he knew of chopping tops at that time, but also noted that "We were in Hollywood, and we didn't go very far." Link Paola was doing similar work in Montrose, north of Glen-

Joe Bailon says Tommy "The Greek" Hrones' '40 Merc was the first custom he ever saw driving the streets of Richmond, in NorCal, in about 1941. Bailon says the top is a Carson, so maybe Tommy picked up the cues in Los Angeles—nosed and decked, teardrop skirts, recessed license, shaved running boards, spinner wheelcovers, later bumpers—it's all there.

Harry Westergard, from Sacramento, is certainly one of the pioneer customizers, but his style is a bit different—more regional—than most think. He started building this '36 for Gene Garrett about 1943. It has a clamshell hood, Packard grille, lights set in the fenders, shaved running boards/rock shields, ripple bumpers, and a padded chopped top with dual rear windows. The '34 Pontiac "vents" in the hood sides were a Sacramento area trend.

dale, before 1940, as were the Bistagnes and likely others. Of Summers, Tom said, "Jimmy Summers was by far the most popular. He was pretty much an icon. He was like a god to us." Tom figures Summers ran his shop near Fairfax High for about 10 years, maybe into the early 1950s.

In a recent discussion with Tony Nancy, he pointed out that Jimmy Summers built the body for his silver, Steve Swaja–designed dragster in

late 1962. At the time his shop was somewhere in the San Fernando Valley. Tony said that Summers passed away just recently.

However, just after the war, it was a pair of near-identical chopped, channeled, and sectioned '39 Ford convertibles parked outside the Olive Hill Garage at Sunset and Vermont in Hollywood that hooked a young Tony Nancy on cars. Owned and built by garage proprietors Art Lellis and Jerry Moffat, the cars (Lellis' was green, Moffat's was gold or bronze) were obviously positioned to attract attention to their business. Nancy would see them as he rode his bicycle by the shop as a teenager, often on his way to Dale Runyan's upholstery shop, where young Nancy apprenticed. Runyan trimmed both '39s, including the padded tops (Lellis' having a unique, three-piece, "panoramic" rear window).

One of the few Westergard cars to use a LaSalle grille was Norm Milne's '38 convertible sedan, seen in front of his gas station, which was the rod and custom hangout in Sacramento after the war. Gene Garrett's '40 is in the background; both cars went to Los Angeles for Carson tops. They were the nucleus of the Thunderbolts club, which included roadsters as well as customs.

Both cars were featured together on the last page of the September 1948 *Hot Rod*, and Lellis' was featured again in May 1950, after the top was added and it was repainted metallic bronze. One of the garage's employees was Chuck Porter, an excellent metalman and pioneer customizer, who ran his own shop in Hollywood for years. Surprisingly, both Lellis' and Moffat's convertibles still exist, as does Porter's well-known chopped and sectioned '50 Ford pickup.

Then there are those who contend that this early custom style originated in Northern California, specifically in Sacramento with Harry Westergard. Westergard died when his new '55 Thunderbird hit a tree late one night at about 100 miles per hour, but at the time he was working for Dick Bertolucci, who was another pioneering customizer in Sacramento. In an interview I did

with Bertolucci in 1989, I asked if Harry Westergard was the originator of "the look": a '36 Ford coupe or roadster with a chopped top, LaSalle grille, solid hood sides, bubble skirts, and '40 Chevy headlights molded into the fenders. He

Most customs evolved with time. This '39 Ford with a Westergard Packard grille, filled hood, and recessed plate, and either a Hall or Carson top, was Mel Falconer's, circa 1946.

Westergard eventually made a steel, lift-off top for Falconer's '39 Ford, filled the rear deck solid, and added solenoids to the shaved doors (possibly a custom first). In this form, owned by Bruce Glenn, it made the May 1954 *R&C*, about the only Westergard car featured in a magazine. It's now in the National Automobile Museum in Reno.

Don't think that all these early customs were Fords or Mercs. Chevys and other GM bodies lent themselves to the style, as well. Jerry Fassett's '47 Chevy convertible, with a Hall top and what are very likely Jimmy Summers' fadeaways molded on, was the handiwork of Westergard and Bertolucci. With a filled hood and deck and inset license plate, it is seen in front of the two-car garage where Westergard worked.

Right middle

This photo, taken in the parking lot of some NorCal circle track by Gene Winfield, shows what many think is the seminal Westergard style: severely chopped top, tall Packard grille, solid hood, ripple bumpers, and long bullet headlights set down low in the front fenders. However, we have no idea who actually built this car.

To wrap up the Sacramento area customs, we have Ed "Buddy" Ohanesian's beautiful '40 Ford convertible sedan, built about 1947. Westergard molded in the '46 Chevy grille, smoothed the hood, and chopped the windshield, then 18-year-old Dick Bertolucci did the rest in a lean-to, including that incredible hand-formed lift-off steel top and the ruby maroon paint job. This is one of my personal favorites.

answered, "I would say Westergard was the originator of that. Westergard did all the custom work in Northern California back then. But most of the guys didn't go for the smooth sides on the hood. They all used '34 Pontiac side panels on '36 Fords— Westergard was the originator. George [Barris, also originally from Sacramento] used to go over and see him all the time. Later we started putting push-button doors in; we'd use Buick solenoids. But Harry is the first person I know of who put solenoids in doors [so the door handles could be shaved]."

Bertolucci figures that Westergard started custom work sometime in the late 1930s. "He was older, you know; about 10 years older than we were." I asked if he had a shop: "No, he did all his work in his garage at home. Matter of fact, it was a chicken coop. It was on Fulton Avenue, near where I lived. He used to do custom work for all the kids around town. I used to go over and see him myself, and talk to him. I was a little bit of a competitor to him, but not much. I was just a kid. He had the name."

Bertolucci started doing custom work in his dad's garage in 1948, when he was about 18. He

Jimmy Summers was doing custom work in his shop on Melrose near Fairfax in Los Angeles before the war, but he built this knockout '40 Mercury convertible around 1947. First painted maroon with a tan Carson top, it is seen here topless in green with a channeled body, raised fenders, sectioned hood, removed running boards/gravel shields, and a handmade grille similar to a Buick's.

The car that most closely resembles what most consider the "Westergard look" is Jack Calori's chopped '36 three-window with a LaSalle grille, clamshell hood, and sunken '40 Chevy headlights. It was built by metalman Herb Reneau of Long Beach in 1947. The louvers are in the hood sides because the small grille opening wouldn't cool it. A local cop, Calori ran a hot '28 roadster on the streets and lakes at the same time. Also shown is a good look at a custom interior of the era.

While customs were built more for style than speed, some did turn up at the dry lakes, where heavy weight wasn't a hindrance and streamlining actually helped. This anonymous postwar Ford with a Lincoln grille, chopped padded top, and full fadeaways was competing at a Russetta Timing Association meet.

said "Westergard was still doing custom work at that time, but then he got out of it. He went to work for a regular body shop, because he couldn't make enough money [doing custom work]. But I stayed in it. I did nothing but custom bodywork from 1948 to 1954."

I asked if there were many "Westergard style" '36 Fords in the Sacramento area: "Yes, quite a few. During the war, Gene Garrett had the first one that I know of. Westergard built it in 1942 or 1943. It had the LaSalle grille and a steel removable hardtop [actually it had a Packard grille]. Now Westergard never did a whole car at one time. Nobody could afford it. In those days we'd just do a little work at a time. A person would bring a car in and you'd do the grille. Next time maybe he'd have the fenders leaded. Then he'd have the headlights changed or the top done. You'd do it in steps."

Of the Barrises in Sacramento, Bertolucci had this to say: "When I was a kid in Sacramento, I guess George and Sam were already starting to do some work, but I didn't know what they did. George had a '36 Ford. He never had it finished—he was just a kid, too. It was all customized, but everything was just welded up; nothing was finished. We did things sort of crude, all of us, to begin with. I got to know him a little bit. But then they left Sacramento, in about 1946 or 1947.

"[George] gives Westergard credit [for teaching him] because Westergard was the only custom man in Sacramento. He saw the things Westergard used to do, and so, like all the rest of us, he'd go home and try to duplicate them. But George Barris used to do all of his work at a little body shop in an alley near 19th and G streets

Continued on page 29

Valley Custom gets short shrift in this chapter, only because it didn't open until 1948. Typical of the clean, crisp look of its earlier customs, the Ray Vega '38 convertible sedan is channeled with '40 front sheetmetal, '41 Stude taillights, '47 bumpers, and a low Carson top.

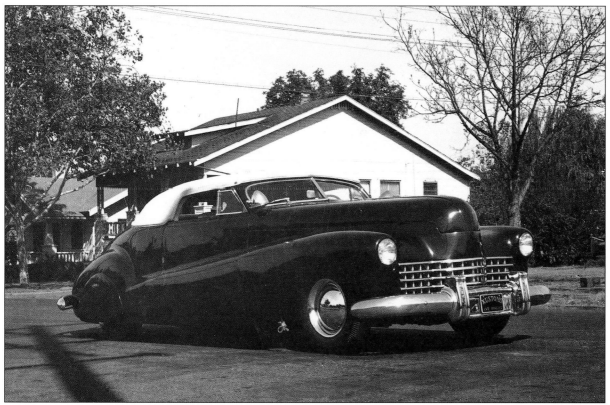

We'll be talking more about the following cars in the next chapter, but they seem to go, visually, more with the cars in this one. After opening his own shop in Los Angeles after the war, the first full custom—the one that established him as a builder— was George Barris' own '41 Buick convertible, to which he added a chopped Carson top, full fadeaway fenders, and a Cad grille.

Sam joined George after he returned from the service after the war. This was Sam's '40 Merc convert, finished strictly in "the style" we're talking about. The photo was taken by Dick Bertolucci on his honeymoon in 1948. The car was little seen because Sam had to sell it to pay bills—a common scenario.

Jesse Lopez' metallic green '41 Ford with a cut-down '48 Cad grille and red Lucite taillights in the bumper guards was another oft-repeated late 1940s Barris style. George even tried to patent the Cad grille. Seen at an outdoor show at Bacon Ford about 1953, it sports sombrero caps, Barris crests, and a Kustoms Los Angeles plaque. Look how straight the body/paint is.

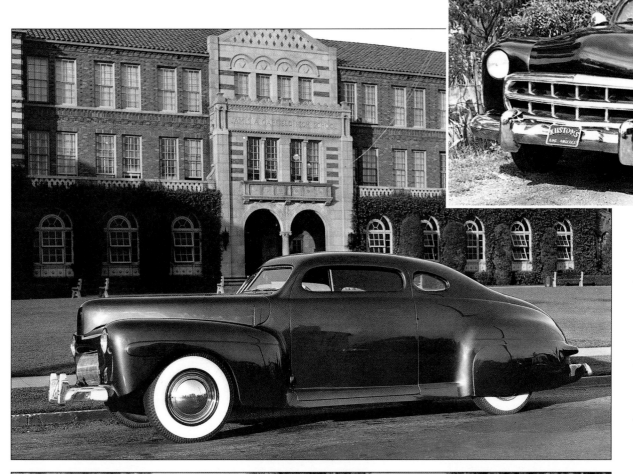

This is Jack Stewart's '41 Ford coupe, discussed in the next chapter. The Ayalas rechopped the top, formed the fadeaways, pancaked the hood, and added the '49 Cad grille.

Left

The Ayala brothers, Gil and Al, opened shop in East Los Angeles sometime in the late 1940s. I doubt they traded notes with the Barrises, but they sure built similar cars. This super smooth and swoopy '42 Ford parked in front of Garfield High was Gil's own, and it epitomizes the postwar custom style. Although it looks darker, the color was listed as "gold" in one program.

Left bottom

The Ayalas were also responsible for this chopped and slightly channeled (sectioned hood) '40 convertible that belonged to well-known hot rod builder John Geraghty in the late 1940s.

This is Gil Ayala's own chopped '40 Merc coupe with full fadeaways and Cad fishtail taillights, which he was more interested in racing on the dry lakes and streets than he was in painting and finishing.

A big turning point for the style of Barris customs was around 1950, when George designed the hardtop look with the curved window frames for Nick Matranga's '40 Merc, and Sam experimented with formed panels from California Metal Shaping to get the smooth flow from roof to trunk seen in this stunning profile. They also cut the windshield less than the top to remove the "squinty" look.

owned by Bruce Brown. He was an old-timer and a great guy, and he used to let all of us use his equipment, like his spray gun, 'cause none of us had anything. And Barris used to go over there and use his place a lot. I'd go over and use his gun and his primer to paint something, and he'd say

'Give me three dollars.' At first, we'd do all the bodywork and get the car ready to paint, then have Bruce Brown spray the enamel for us."

What Dick Bertolucci would never say in an interview is that his own metalwork, paint, and detail was as good as, if not better than,

And we can't close this chapter without showing Joe Bailon's tour de force that launched his career, the *Miss Elegance* '41 Chevy coupe.

There were variations on the theme, but the Barris style was pretty well set. Both painted forest green, with the creases removed from the fenders, Bill "De Carr" Ortega's '41 has a '47 Olds grille and fadeaways, while Snooky Janich's has a '46 Chevy grille.

any other customizer in the field. His candy paint jobs are legendary. He excelled at drag and Bonneville racing in the early days with GMC sixes, and is now doing it again at the nostalgia drags. His collection of restored Chevrolets has won countless Vintage Chevy Club of America awards. And, though he is now semi-retired, his Bertolucci Body and Fender shop remains one of the largest—and best—in the Sacramento area.

Meanwhile, over in the Oakland area on the east side of the San Francisco Bay, this Carson style of customizing was getting going before the war. Some guy named Hall, supposedly a former employee at Carson's, opened Hall's Top Shop and was building chopped, padded tops identical to Carson's. In addition, Joe Bailon, who didn't really start in the business until he returned from the service during World War II, said he saw the first custom of this type driving on the streets of Richmond, California (just north of Oakland), in 1941 or so. It was a '39 or '40 Mercury convertible owned by famed pinstriper Tommy "The Greek" Hrones. The Mercury was black with a chopped (supposedly) Carson top, lowered, and had bubble skirts. The car was totally dechromed other than door handles, the running boards had been removed, the license recessed, and it ran wide whites with full moon wheelcovers and what appear to be stock bumpers. Bailon said, "His was about the only chopped custom in the Oakland area then. I have no idea where he got his ideas."

Unfortunately, Tommy is 88 years old as this is written, and he couldn't tell me much about the car other than a bodyman named Al Tinnini (Tininni?) did the metalwork. But it seems surprising that Tommy's custom Merc could be so similar to the Southern California style—it lacked only ripple bumpers—that early on. The Oakland area customs had their own regional styling and Lord knows, when Joe Bailon, Oakland's best-known customizer, got back from the war and started building a chopped '41 Chevy coupe, he didn't follow the style of the car that first inspired him—not by a long shot.

The Renegades were a very active custom car club from the Long Beach area in the 1950s and early 1960s. Larry Watson striped many of their cars and Ed Schelhaas, a local bodyman who did the custom work on Larry's *Grapevine* Chevy, did custom work for them, including Saint Vasques' '50 Chevy convertible, which has a floating De Soto grille, Cad headlights, Olds windshield, Packard taillights, and a chopped Carson top.

THE CLASSIC CUSTOM CAR ERA

LIKE HOT RODDING,

the building of custom cars increased rapidly after the end of World War II. In fact, it is my strong contention that the decade of roughly 1947–1957 is the real custom car era. It started with cars like '36 Fords, '39–'41 Fords and Mercs, and '40–'47 Chevys.

While the teenagers were raising hell on the streets in hopped-up, fenderless Model T, Model A, and Deuce roadsters, the older rodders, especially those returning from the service with some pay in their pockets and good jobs to look forward to, were eyeing newer, more reliable, and more comfortable cars with amenities like roll-up windows, and they were trying to figure how to personalize—customize—them.

As we saw in Chapter 1, the style had already been set before the war: smoothing, dechroming, lowering, top-chopping, fender-skirting, and so on. It was natural. It's what these more modern cars called for. It was nearly intuitive. It had to be, because there were no magazines to publicize the latest trends until after 1948, and even then the fledgling *Hot Rod* paid far less attention to customs than it did to rods and race cars. This was natural, since the custom contingent has always been a relatively small fraction of the rodding world. But somehow the word spread that ripple bumpers, spinner hubcaps, Buick teardrop skirts, wide whitewalls, and Appleton spotlights were the parts to have on your custom.

Of course, the Carson Top Shop had as much work as it could handle after the war. In fact, the shop's owner, Bob Hauser, estimated that in its heyday through 1948, the shop was averaging 15 tops a week. By the late 1940s, Bill Gaylord of Bell, California, was installing similar tops, too, along with custom upholstery.

Although the story sometimes changes with the telling, George Barris said his brother Sam joined the navy in 1941 (or 1943). Some time after that, George Barris moved to Los Angeles in the '36 Ford convertible he had built in Sacramento, and went to work at the Jones Body, Fender & Paint shop at Florence and Main, south of downtown Los Angeles. It was primarily a repair shop, but he started doing, and bringing in, custom work, which they encouraged. By late 1944, said Barris, he opened his own small shop on Imperial Highway in Bell,

One-day, outdoor car shows at new car dealers' or other parking lots were the norm before the big, indoor, judged shows began being staged after 1950. This one, at Bacon Ford, was obviously 1953 or later.

and when Sam was discharged a year later, Barris convinced him to join him. Then, after (or before) moving to a slightly larger shop at 7674 Compton Ave. in southeast Los Angeles, Barris built a '41 Buick convertible, to which he added full fadeaway fenders (not seen on stock Buicks until the '42–'45 Roadmaster), a '42 Cadillac grille, a low Carson top, frenched headlights, and a rich royal metallic maroon paint job (Barris' first). This car was supposedly the only custom at the first SCTA Hot Rod Show at the Los Angeles armory in 1948, and it was on the cover of a young *Road and Track* in May 1948. Barris claims this car "really put us on the map." It definitely

presaged a longer, lower, more streamlined style of custom, especially as turned out by the Barris shop.

Barris was also one of the first advertisers in *Hot Rod* magazine, first as "Barris's Custom Shop," later as Barris' Custom Shop—Kustom Automobiles. In the first *HRM* were also ads for Jimmy Summers, Eastern Auto Supply (advertising solid hood sides, grilles and fill-ins, and Hollywood running board trim), and Carson Top Shop. Later in 1948, Link's Custom Shop (Link Paola) was added, as well.

I'm not sure when the Ayala Brothers shop on Olympic Blvd. in East Los Angeles opened, because I never met Gil or Al Ayala. Both have been dead more than a decade, and nobody who knew them closely or worked there seems to be around. But they had to have been in operation before 1949, because Los Angeles Roadsters member Jack Stewart had them doing work on his custom '41 Ford coupe by then. Stewart said that the Ayalas were much like George and Sam Barris, in that Gil Ayala was "the front man and painter" (like George Barris) and that Al Ayala "was one of the best metalmen" he knew (like Sam Barris). Stewart also surmises, I think correctly, that in both cases the "frontman" owned the business, while the other brother was an

hourly employee. Stewart said that Gil "was a real likable guy," and Joe Bailon has spoken similarly.

Stewart also said that the Ayalas were among the first to make full fadeaway fenders (as Ayala did on his own '40 Merc coupe and Stewart's car), and that they were the first he saw make cardboard templates for body panels and have them formed in sheet metal by California Metal Shaping, "instead of layering on tons of lead." Stewart

Having already cut so many 1939–1948 FoMoCo products, the new '49 Mercury wasn't much of a challenge for Sam Barris, who put the torch to his own new Merc as soon as he got it. One nice touch he gave his car was removing the "hump" from the door and downturn at the rear quarter to give it a full fadeaway fender line.

35

At the same time that Sam was cutting his own Merc, the Ayala brothers were doing this one for Louie Bettancourt. With its slanted B-pillar, full-fadeaway fender line, extended headlights, rounded hood corners, and single, simple chrome spear, I think this is the smoothest, cleanest, most streamlined of all the early chopped Mercs. The Barrises finished it up with custom frenched taillights, a grille of '54 Ford parts, and deep burgundy wine paint.

Below
There's not a whole lot done to Jerry Quesnel's seldom-seen '49 other than the top chop—but what a chop! Done in 1951, you can tell Sam was experimenting with such things as the slanted B-pillar. I don't think he cut any '49–'51 lower than this.

said Kenny Lucas first chopped the top on his Ford, but Ayala rechopped it using formed panels. Stewart and a friend channeled the body about 6 inches in the backyard, then the Ayalas pancaked the hood, added a '49 Cad grille, installed '48 Ford front fenders, and made the fadeaways.

Stewart mentioned that he met George Barris in 1945, and they were friends. So I asked why he took his car to Ayalas' shop instead. He answered that Barris would take in too many cars, and they wouldn't get done for quite a while. But it seems that there were several instances when the big work would get done at one shop, and the finishing touches at the other. In Stewart's case, he took his Ford to Barris' to have the trunk corners rounded, the red plastic taillights formed, the door jambs cleaned up, and then the metallic bronze lacquer applied. After pausing for a couple of minutes, Stewart recalled that the reason he had to do this was because Gil Ayala, who liked speed and street racing, had been caught running 100 miles per hour on the street and then trying to flee to Mexico, and had to spend about three months in jail.

Stewart also recalled that the very small building in front of the shop, that I called the office in my "Shop Tour" article in *The Rodder's Journal* Number 4, was actually the House of Chrome custom accessory shop, which advertised such things as solid hood sides, Appleton spots, fender skirts, ripple disks, chrome fender shields, and such things in 1948 issues of *Hot Rod*. Its address was 4084 E. Olympic, and Ayala's was 4074.

I asked Stewart, who has been a '32 Ford roadster-type rodder for decades, why he built a custom at that time. He replied that in high school (he graduated from Los Angeles' South

Gate High in 1947) he first had a hot rod, "just like Art Chrisman's (who went to nearby Compton High at about the same time)—a '36 Ford four-door sedan." I said that Chrisman's, though it had a hot flathead, was more of a custom: lowered in the back, teardrop skirts, ripple bumpers, and so on. Stewart said, "Yeah, just like that." Then he went on, "Customs were in then. They were the going thing until the Korean War started. Then the bottom dropped out. After 1950–1951, young guys were being drafted and sent overseas, and older guys were getting married and getting out of cars. The drive-ins, the cruising, all that stopped. Besides, the '49–'51 Mercs were coming in, and our cars were outdated." In 1951, Stewart sold his custom '41 for $2,800 to Jim Skonzakis of Ohio (who also

Convertibles are easier to chop than coupes, so it's surprising that Ralph Testa's was the first the Barrises did. With '49 Buick taillights turned sideways in the rear fenders and a cut-down Henry J grille, George says he painted it coral blue-purple.

Rev. Larry Ernst, a Catholic priest from a well-to-do family in Toledo, Ohio, bought this '51 Chevy Bel Air hardtop new, with Continental kit, and immediately drove it to the Barrises to have it chopped and customized. It may be the first curved-glass Chevy they did, but they did it beautifully, streamlining the whole car and extending the rear fenders to hide the spare tire. It was purple and lavender this time around.

Then came the Hirohata Merc. It was the first '51 the Barrises chopped, it was the first to use the Buick side chrome, and it reprised the Matranga hardtop with curved window frames—plus so much more. This is an obvious turning point in customizing, when builders are starting to think more is better, influenced in no small part by car show judging. On this car, however, it all works.

least in the lower-priced lines—were offered until 1949. The early 1940s cars were really cheap (and used). An excellent way to spruce up one of these old cars was to take it to a custom shop for a newer look, new paint, and plush new threads.

Several things happened right around 1950 that had a major impact on customizing. First was the Barris Brothers' creation of the Nick Matranga '40 Mercury. Sam Barris worked for most of a year creating the gently sloping rear roofline, the hardtop treatment with the curved side window glass frames (which would later be repeated on the Hirohata Merc), and the slightly enlarged windshield to remove the "squinty" look of previous chopped Fords and Mercs. Compare this car to the Zaro/Andril Mercs (two earlier Barris cars shown in Chapter One), and you will see a smoother, more refined custom style emerging.

Second, of course, was the introduction of the '49–'51 Mercury; probably nothing had as much

Frank Sonzogni was a Lynwood policeman who moonlighted with a torch and lead paddle in the Barris shop. He gave his own Merc a fender line/rear quarter scoop somewhat similar to the Hirohata's. In two-tone green, it had a '54 De Soto grille and '52 De Soto bumpers. The pinstriping doesn't exactly enhance the package.

bought the *Kookie Kar* and owned the *Golden Sahara*), who showed it throughout the Midwest and East for years, until it got hit by a train. Miraculously, it was restored by Bob Drake of Indiana, who still owns and drives it.

Before we look at the changes that occurred around 1950, I want to point out one big factor that pushed the customs' popularity right after the war: New cars had not been manufactured at all from 1943 until 1946, and no new models—at

This is the second version of the Fred Rowe Barris '51 convertible, with Buick side trim and scoops added, and real Chrysler wire wheels. In this form it appeared with the Hirohata Merc in the movie *Running Wild*. It was located about 10 years ago and very nicely restored.

Designer Harry Bradley critiqued the Dave Bugarin '51 Barris Merc in a recent article, but I've always liked the '53 Buick headlights, the hardtop treatment, and especially the '54 Packard taillights. Remember, these are all parts from new or nearly new cars at the time. George called the colors organic and blue fog metallic.

impact on customizing, as we're discussing it, as this vehicle, which we will cover at some length in a moment. Third was the institution of judged, competitive car shows, beginning with the Oakland Roadster Show in January 1950, and continuing with Petersen's Motorama in Los Angeles, the Indianapolis car show, the Hartford Autorama, and countless others. This eventually did two things: It caused custom (and rod) owners to quit driving their cars on the street, to keep them pristine for show judging. And it spurred custom owners to continually rebuild their cars, adding more and more point-winning modifications. We will discuss this phenomenon at length in the next chapter.

But let's look at the sizable effect the '49–'51 Mercury had on this decade of customizing. To do

The last of the "original radical custom Mercs" was Buddy Alcorn's, built in 1955 and finished in a deep eggplant purple-maroon. He traded it two years later for a new, mild custom '57 Ford.

Custom upholsterer Bill Gaylord bought this '53 Olds as a burn-out. He cut the roof off and has fully customized it at least twice. This second version has Packard taillights; full tuck-and-roll interior; and a "cantilever" padded, lift-off top that is a Gaylord trademark.

so, I will once again call upon an essay written by noted automotive designer (and custom car owner) Harry Bentley Bradley, titled "'49–'51 Merc Customs—A Styling Critique" that first appeared in an obscure custom car magazine in 1985, and which I reprinted in the February 1991 issue of *Rod & Custom*, along with a panel listing a dozen of "The Original Radical Custom Mercs." In it he said:

A small fleet of incredible Mercurys, customized in Los Angeles during the early 1950s, has forever identified the '49–'51 Mercury as *the* all-time custom. Why this particular car and these particular customs?

Of the postwar designs, Mercury's was certainly not the most modern. Its 1949 styling was a tentative combination of old and new that was not as fresh as its sister cars from Ford and Lincoln nor its competition from General Motors. [In fact, the '49 Mercury was slated to be the new Ford for that year, but the company realized that it wasn't new enough, and designed the revolutionary slab-sided, flat-hood, "shoebox" '49 Ford at the last minute as a substitute.] Some of the dated items included:

• Long roof (especially for coupes) and short, slumping deck.
• Two-piece, V-shaped windshield
• Small windows and thick lower body proportions
• Old-style fadeaway front fenders
• Rounded, prewar back-end styling with fenders that did not extend beyond the deck lid
• Clamshell doors on the sedan

Mercury tried to correct some of these problems in 1951 by extending the rear fenders and enlarging the rear window, but this was too little too late.

Ironically, the styling flaws that made Mercury less than new in the showroom were exactly what made the car so appealing to customizers. Virtually every line and shape was familiar to the Los Angeles custom shops that had been working with the '40–'48 Fords and Mercs for nearly a decade. Chopping the V-windshield was much easier than chopping GM's new curved designs. When chopped, the small windows and thick pillars had the familiar, sinister custom look. The long Mercury roof could be given the same flowing sweep into the rounded deck as the earlier cars had. A dechromed and lowered new Mercury back end also looked very much like the earlier customs. The low front fenders and tall hood were much preferred over Ford's higher, boxy fender line and nearly flat hood. And, strangely, Mercury's add-on fender skirts seemed more "custom" than GM's flush skirts.

To the customizer, the '49 Merc was the perfect car, just waiting for the torch. Beginning in the late 1930s, Southern California customizing had developed a certain style initially intended to modernize the fat, rounded bodies of later 1930s and 1940s cars. While the '49 Mercury failed to break new styling ground, it brilliantly reworked older design themes in a way that presented an excellent opportunity for customizers at precisely the time when they had developed their repertoire of styling and metalworking skills.

The custom cars of all time were the first chopped '49–'51 Mercs, as listed in an accompanying chart. These stunning cars didn't just happen. They were the result of a decade of customizing tradition that preceded them. That cultish tradition included:

• Lowering the car through suspension, frame, body, and roof surgery.
• Removing chrome and emblems to let the body styling dominate
• Molding separate, assembled parts into one flowing statement
• Extensively and appropriately using parts from other cars, such as grilles, bumpers, and taillights
• Applying deep, organic, hand-rubbed colors to accent the forms

In those days of the 1940s and 1950s, customizers didn't destroy the organic design or build completely new segments of a car. Instead, they improved a car by emphasizing its good points and correcting its weaknesses. The early Mercs and the 1940s customs that preceded them were handsome automobiles with well-proportioned, coherent body and fender forms that the customizers respected and blended together into dramatic automotive statements.

Left
Hershel "Junior" Conway was just 17 when he, his brother, and the Barris shop modified this tasty, mild '50 Ford daily driver. Doing the paint prep in his driveway earned him a job as a "sand boy" at Barris', which eventually led to chief painter. Today he is one of the best automotive painters in the world.

The Original Radical Custom Mercs

Year and Model	Owner	Customizer	Year Built
1949 coupe	Sam Barris	Sam and George Barris	1950
1949 coupe	Louie Bettancourt	Gil and Al Ayala	1950
Same car	John Zupan	Sam and George Barris	1956
1949 coupe	Jerry Quesnel	Sam and George Barris	1951
1950 coupe	Wally Welch	Gil and Al Ayala	1951
Same car	repainted	Sam and George Barris	1953
1950 convertible	Ralph Testa	Sam and George Barris	1951
1951 coupe	Bob Hirohata	Sam and George Barris	1952
1951 convertible	Fred Rowe	Sam and George Barris	1953
1951 coupe	Frank Sonzogni	Frank Sonzogni	1954
1951 coupe	Dave Bugarin	Sam and George Barris	1955
1950 coupe	Buddy Alcorn	Sam and George Barris	1955

There will be some unavoidable overlapping throughout this book. But in the second half of this classic custom era, we see the same cars being reworked with more intricate side chrome, multicolor paint jobs, more scoops with more chrome teeth, more cluttered grilles, and so on, usually to the car's detriment. This was done initially because, as the cars were driven on the street, they would get chipped or scratched, and sometimes dented or wrecked, and the multilayer lacquer paint jobs or sometimes hasty or crude bodywork would crack or check. But more often, as we shall explore in the next chapter, the changes were made to garner more show points for the upcoming season and/or because the car was sold to a new owner, who wanted to upgrade it or add his personal touches to it. Examples of such redos would include the 1952 and 1953 versions of the Rev. Larry Ernst '51 Chevy by Barris, including three-tone paint, the Johnny Zupan version of the Bettancourt Merc, and the *New Grecian* Studebaker by Barris. What we are seeing as the decade progresses are street customs morphing into show cars.

But what really brought a screeching halt to the classic custom car era were the new cars from Detroit, beginning subtly in 1955–1956, and exploding with fins, scoops, wraparound windshields, and so on in 1957–1958. These cars simply killed customizing as we knew it in the periods before and after World War II. Park a chopped, lowered, leaded, and lacquered '40 or '50 Merc next to a '54 Dodge, and which car will win the "wow!" contest? Now park the same

Continued on page 47

Far left
Jay Johnston's Ford, seen in 1954, was the most radically chopped shoebox of the era. Built from pieces by him and friend Bill Bowman, they grafted a much-cut hardtop roof to a convertible body to get this profile. Gaylord outdid himself on the pink and white interior, featuring a chromed '51 dash, column, moldings, and some classic '50s cheesecake.

One body style that lends itself best to the sectioning process is the shoebox Ford, and Ron Dunn's, cut by Valley Custom, was probably the first and most famous. Valley Custom was known for the simplicity of its cars, and this one is a prime example.

THE CUSTOM CAR MAGAZINES

There have never been many car magazines devoted strictly to customs. In fact there are only two from the early days: Petersen's *Custom Cars,* (1957) and *Customs Illustrated* (1958) out of New York. Another "little book" was titled *Custom Craft*, out of Canton, Ohio, but it was neither customs-only nor long-lived.

However, plenty of rod-type magazines featured custom cars. *Hot Rod* showed pictures of customs, beginning with its first (January 1948) issue. Even though it is shown racing at the lakes (and labeled a "Competition Coupe"), Bob Pierson's '36 three-window on the August 1948 cover is ostensibly a custom, with its teardrop skirts and ripple bumpers. Then, beginning in the September 1948 issue, *HRM* began featuring custom cars on its last page, the first pair being Art Lellis' and Jerry Moffatt's chopped and channeled '39 Ford convertibles from Hollywood. One of the more surprising customs featured on the last page that first year was Ray Giovannoni's from Washington, D.C. (later of Giovannoni Cams fame). What is surprising is that it is done in the so-called "Westergard style": teardrop skirts, molded running boards, solid hood sides, Packard grille, what appear to be Buick headlights molded down in the fenders, '41 Ford bumpers, single-bar flippers, Appleton spots, a chopped windshield, and a black (or some other dark color) glossy paint job—a stunning car. The text says he did the work himself, then drove it to Los Angeles to have the padded top (we assume a Carson) added. How was this style known to an East Coast customizer before it appeared in any national magazines?

What a lot of people don't realize is that *Motor Trend*, which Petersen launched in September 1949, carried quite a bit of custom coverage in the beginning, including striking covers of well-known cars such as the Hirohata Merc and the Ernst Chevy. In fact, *MT* was more-or-less the Petersen custom car magazine until the emphasis began shifting more to new car coverage. Then, surprisingly, in 1957 *MT* began featuring current customs again, including a "new eight-page section—Custom Cars Illustrated" in the May 1957 issue, obviously intended to help launch the new *Custom Cars* magazine in September 1957.

At the same time (mid-1950s), *Motor Life* magazine, listed as a Quinn Publication, but at the Petersen address, was pushing custom car articles, especially how-tos, seemingly in competition with *Motor Trend*. *Motor Life* actually began as the little *Hop Up* magazine at Quinn, then changed names as it went to large size when Quinn started the little *Rod & Custom*.

The one magazine that has featured customs the most consistently over the years is, of course, *Rod & Custom*. Its very first (May 1953) issue (actually titled *Rods and Customs* for that issue only) was nearly half custom cars, including some of the best of the day, ranging from Rev. Ernst's Chevy and Ron Dunn's '50 Ford, to a Dean Batchelor photo feature on prewar customs. In subsequent years, the mix in *R&C* tended to be heavier on rods than customs, but that reflected the audience mix (the custom car crowd has always been smaller than the hot rod contingent—that's just the way it is). However, *R&C* always showed the best customs of the day, including Editor Spence Murray's amazing *Dream Truck* project. And while customs tended to disappear from the more mainstream rod mags in the 1960s and 1970s, *R&C* continued to feature cars like Bill Hines' *Lil Bat* (1959), Chuck Atwood's *My Blue Heaven* (1960), Mike Budnick's A-Bros. '60 Pontiac (1963), Cliff Inman's Wilhelm '57 Chrysler (1964), Rod Powell's chopped Merc (1965), and even Bob Huffman's radical '65 Chevy (1969). Of course, the big problem is that *R&C* was gone for most of the 1970s and 1980s, before it could resume featuring custom cars when it finally returned in December 1988.

The other Petersen title that catered largely to custom cars was *Car Craft* (Petersen bought *R&C* from Quinn Publications in July 1955; *Car Craft* started as *Honk*—a Petersen title—and switched to *Car Craft* in December 1953). The early issues were a mix of rods, customs, and racing of various types, with the subtitle "The Show-How Magazine" on the contents page. Sometime between March 1955 and July 1955 (my collection is not complete) Dick Day became editor and the slant leaned a little more toward customs. By the November 1956 issue, the subtitle switched to "The Custom Car Magazine." By October 1957 it was back to the "Show-How" mag, but still featuring about the same number of customs, with Dick Day the editor through the July 1962 issue. For a brief time (1961–1962) it was combined with *Kart* magazine, but during that time it also presented the "10 Best Customs" annually. *Car Craft* ran sporadic custom features through 1964 (interestingly, one of the last was Jim "Bones" Noteboom's Winfield '64 Riviera in the October 1964 issue) but from 1965 on, it was essentially a drag racing mag, which it remains today.

As mentioned, Petersen launched *Custom Cars* magazine in September 1957, unfortunately about half a decade too late. Dick Day served double duty, editing this new title at the same time that he was doing *Car Craft*. This is by far the best custom car magazine produced, being completely custom-oriented and featuring all the heavy hitters of the 1950s: Junior, Bugarin, St. Vasquez, Goulart, Sahagon, Kopper Kart, Hocker, Sonzogni, Alcorn, Lyle Lake, Bailon, Tiago, Watson, Halicki, Hines, you name it. I'm not sure exactly when it went away—the last issue I have is August 1960—but I'm sure it died for lack of custom-specific advertising, a problem that persists today.

Now, what about those little "Eastern" magazines? Other than the aforementioned *Customs Illustrated*, arguably the best of the lot, these magazines featured rods, customs, and drag racing. In chronological order, they would include: *Rodding and Restyling* (1955–1961) from Canton, Ohio; *Rod Builder & Customizer* (1956–1957) from Washington, D.C.; *Custom Rodder* (1957–1959) from Canton, Ohio, and later New York—not to be confused with the much later mag of the same name from

Given today's version, few would guess *Motor Trend* catered to customs from its inception in 1949 through early 1958, as seen here. New car tests and sports cars were also mixed in. Even early *Road and Track* featured customs, such as the May 1948 issue, which had Barris' first Buick on the cover.

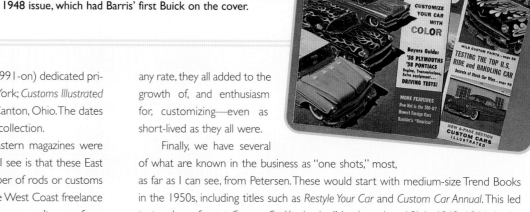

McMullen/Primedia, being the only contemporary magazine (1991-on) dedicated primarily to customs; *Car Speed & Style* (1957–1959) from New York; *Customs Illustrated* (1958–1961) from New York; and *Custom Craft* (1960) from Canton, Ohio. The dates given are the best approximations I can make given my own collection.

Some contend, not necessarily accurately, that these Eastern magazines were inferior, and that they featured ugly cars. The biggest problem I see is that these East Coast/Midwest mags just didn't have anywhere near the number of rods or customs available to photograph that the West Coast mags did. Plus the West Coast freelance photographers were tied to West Coast publications, and there weren't many freelancers elsewhere in the country. Finally, several of these magazines were produced by publishers who saw that West Coast hot rod and custom car magazines were selling in big numbers, and wanted to get in on the action without really understanding the subject matter. Some were just bad magazines. Others—*Customs Illustrated*, *Rodding and Restyling*, *Rod Builder & Customizer*, and *Car Speed & Style*—were pretty good. At

any rate, they all added to the growth of, and enthusiasm for, customizing—even as short-lived as they all were.

Finally, we have several of what are known in the business as "one shots," most, as far as I can see, from Petersen. These would start with medium-size Trend Books in the 1950s, including titles such as *Restyle Your Car* and *Custom Car Annual*. This led to two large-format *Custom Car Yearbooks* (Numbers 1 and 2) in 1963–1964. At the same time (1962–1963) there was a series of little "Spotlight Books," most nominally authored by George Barris, with titles such as *Scoops and Sculpturing*, *Headlights and Fenders*, *Dashboards and Detailing*, and so on. There were at least nine of these pertaining to custom cars.

And then, before the close of the 1960s, they were all gone.

Continued on next page

Between 1955 and 1961 several "Eastern" small-size magazines featuring rods and customs came and went. The Plymouth on the *Rodding and Restyling* cover is New York customizer Herb Gary's personal car. *Customs Illustrated* was one of the last and best. The issue with Ron Courtney's finned Ford on the cover was the first car mag I ever bought—because of that amazing car.

From 1953 to present day, the magazine showing the most custom cars would have to be *Rod & Custom*, though it switched to street rods in the late 1960s and early 1970s, then was gone for most of the 1970s and 1980s. The car on this cover is from Indiana's "finmaster," Bob Metz.

Although it covered rods and racing, *Car Craft* was heavily into customs and custom how-tos through the 1950s and barely into the 1960s. Then it became a drag racing mag.

Plus there was a run of small-size Spotlite Books under the *Hot Rod* banner in the early 1960s, most showing how-to projects photographed by George Barris.

Motor Life, originally a Quinn publication competing with *Motor Trend*, also carried a lot of custom content in the 1950s, and some great covers, such as the Barris shop scene.

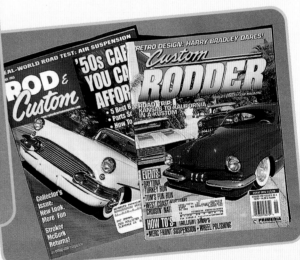

The only Petersen periodical devoted strictly to custom cars was—what else?—*Custom Cars* magazine, which ran monthly from 1957 to 1960. But it came too late, and lacked advertising support.

Petersen's early medium-size *Custom Cars* Annuals were under the *Motor Trend* banner. Then in 1963 and 1964 only, they produced *Hot Rod Custom Car Yearbook* Numbers 1 and 2.

Although custom cars revived substantially in the last two decades of the 1900s, by the turn of the century the only two magazines featuring customs regularly were *R&C* and the new *Custom Rodder*.

Continued from page 43

custom next to a '57 or '58 Dodge. See what I mean? The Exner-designed Mopar fin-mobiles were the most far-out, by a long shot. But even cars like the '57 Ford or Chevy were stealing the show from traditional customs. And I contend that the '58 Impala was an out-and-out factory custom. This radically redesigned, one-year model was suddenly longer, wider, and lower than its boxy predecessors. The new X-style frame essentially allowed the body to be channeled. It had scoops in the quarters and a scoop on the roof. It was nearly nosed and decked. And even the upholstery mimicked custom tuck-and-roll designs.

I'm not saying that custom cars suddenly went away, by any means. But these new cars of the latter 1950s didn't need to be chopped, channeled, molded, or sectioned. All these cars needed was maybe a little

dechroming, lowering, a flashy custom paint job, and some accessories like chrome wheels and lakes pipes. These cars immediately made the traditional custom Fords, Mercs, and Chevrolets obsolete.

Perhaps the most famous Valley Custom section job, and its most famous custom car, was Jack Stewart's *Polynesian* '50 Olds from Canton, Ohio, which was featured in many magazines, but was afforded a 47-page full buildup sequence in the 1954 *Motor Trend Custom Cars Annual*. Painted a rich maroon, it epitomizes the clean '50s Valley Custom Style.

Speaking of clean style, how about Buster Litton's '49 Ford club coupe? This is one of the best custom shoeboxes ever built, with graceful lines and perfect proportions. Plus, it's unique. Originally chopped by Barris, the rest of the car was done in George Cerny's shop, probably with metalwork by his brother Carl. The fronts of the fenders are '51 Stude, the rear quarters are '51 Olds 98, and the top has been cut to hardtop style. The color is cocoa rust.

We mustn't forget the *Dream Truck* in this chapter of custom history. Belonging to *Rod & Custom*'s first editor, Spence Murray, it was modified by many people over several years in the pocket-size pages of the magazine. Sam Gates chopped the in-the-crate new '54 cab. Valley Custom sectioned it (of course). Winfield sectioned the hood and front fenders. Barris added the hood scoop, headlights, and front and rear pans/grilles. Finally Bob Metz of Indiana built the fins.

As we have mentioned, '40 Fords can be built as rods or customs. Tom Hocker's, from Oakland, is definitely a custom with a chopped top, molded fenders, filled hood, shaved body, and frenched headlights, all by Barris. Later it was converted to quad headlights, but retained its metallic blue with light blue scallops paint scheme.

Another typical Barris custom of the classic era was Chuck DeWitt's '50 Ford convertible from Long Beach. Painted a deep purple with '52 Buick and '53 Olds side chrome, and a scoop in front of the Mercury skirt, it ran 118 at the lakes with a 296-inch flathead before it was customized. Then it was featured driving to Bonneville with editor Dick Day in the December 1953 *Car Craft*.

About 1956 Johnny Zupan bought the Bettancourt Merc and took it to Barris for some "updating." Barris added more side chrome, scooped skirts, some funky wheelcovers with stars around them, and painted the lower half gold with gold scallops around the grille and headlights. Then Dean Jeffries went wild striping it, especially on the dash, which included "weirdo" scenes on the glovebox and heater. Olds-powered, by 1970 it was on jackstands in Jeffries' lot when someone dragged it away, sans wheels, and it's never been seen since.

Let's look at four examples. Buddy Alcorn, who paid Barris a few thousand dollars to build his chopped '50 Merc in 1955, traded that car straight across for Dick Jackson's very mildly customized, new '57 Ford. All this car had was a '54 Chevy grille, mild dechroming, mildly reworked headlights and taillights, a custom paint job with pinstripe scallops, some minor custom upholstery, and accessories like Lancer wheelcovers, lakes pipes, and spot lights. After painting some scallops on it, Jackson quickly got rid of the

Continued on page 53

A bit atypical for Bailon, Elton Kantor's smooth, swoopy '50 Ford was also a convertible (like Jay Johnston's) with a very chopped Victoria top grafted on. Painted dark metallic blue, it won the Elegance Award at Oakland in 1953.

Another well-known member of the Renegades was Duane Steck and his home-built chopped '54 Chevy *Moonglow*. It is shown here in its third and final iteration, in 1960, with hooded headlights, molded grille, and Watson candy blue paint. Note tow-bar mounts under the bumper for taking it to shows. A couple of years later, he traded it for a sports car, and by the end of the decade it was crushed.

Let's travel up north, where Joe Bailon was plenty busy moving customs through his shop in the East Bay area. This was Joe's first shop, in San Leandro in 1950, and that's him leaning on a primered *Miss Elegance* on the left.

Similar to the Renegades in Long Beach, the Satan's Angels of Hayward was the Bay Area custom car club of the era. Members shown here include Frank Livingston, Jerry Sahagon, Eddie Dameral, and Sonny Morris. Bailon built all of these cars but one.

Bailon's first version of Livingston's fastback Chevy, in gold, included a '56 Plymouth grille, '50 Chrysler taillights in extended fenders, and frenched headlights. In a second version seen on the January 1958 *Car Craft* cover, Joe added several fender scoops and chrome teeth, while Mel Pinoli gave it technically the first candy paint job, in tropic tangerine orange over Brazilian gold. Unfortunately, he mixed these colors with printer's dyes, and they faded immediately.

The first Bailon candy red paint job, mixed with automotive paint toners, was sprayed on Jerry Sahagon's semi custom '51 Chevy, as seen here. The grille is typical Bailon. This car later had a chopped top and canted quad lights, and Sahagon is still doing custom upholstery today.

The *Candy Bird*, built for Joe Castro in 1958, may be Bailon's most famous custom. It features Joe's characteristic sculptured chrome bar grilles and chrome-toothed scoops, along with handmade sidepipes and nerfs, and is finished in candy red with small gold scallops and Tommy the Greek striping.

Continued from page 49

Merc in favor of a '57 T-Bird that he modified in very similar fashion to his former Ford.

In 1959 a 16-year-old Jim McNiel was able to buy the well-used Hirohata Merc off the back row of a used car lot for $500. "Dirty" Doug Kinney had traded it in on a brand-new '59 Cadillac that he lowered, painted, and added custom wheels and pipes to.

Sometime in the early 1960s, Duane Steck traded the *Moonglow* '54 Chevy for a sports car. His brother, Steve, spotted its stripped hulk at the appropriately named Terminal Island scrap yards near the Los Angeles harbor a few years later, and was able to salvage one of the blue Plexiglas wind wings before he watched it go through the crusher.

And Mox Miller's '58 Impala, which he bought new and immediately customized, was able to win the semi custom class at car shows even though it did not have a single body modification on it. It even had all of its original chrome and emblems. What made it a winning custom was its panel paint job by Dick Jackson with outline striping by Dennis Ricklefs, its fully chromed undercarriage, full tuck-and-roll interior, polished mag wheels, and supercharged and chromed 348 engine. But to demonstrate what an all-out show car this vehicle was (and is), the engine has never been started nor the car driven since it was built in its current configuration in 1962. It had to be hand-pushed in and out of shows.

Before I close this chapter I must mention the growing number of custom shops that evolved during the 1950s and into the 1960s, especially with the proliferation of custom car or rod and custom magazines, including the early *Motor Trend*, the originally custom-oriented *Car Craft* (beginning in

1953), and the short-lived *Custom Cars* from Petersen 1957–1960). The well-known shops would include Barris in Lynwood, George Cerny in Compton, Dean Jeffries in Hollywood, Gil and Al Ayala in East Los Angeles, Valley Custom in Burbank, Joe Wilhelm in San Jose, Dick Bertolucci in Sacramento, Joe Bailon in Hayward, Gene Winfield in Modesto, and Bill Cushenbery in Monterey, to name some in California alone. In other parts of the country were Darryl Starbird and Dave Stuckey in Wichita, Kansas; the Alexander Brothers and Bill Hines in Detroit, Michigan; Herb Gary in Sea Cliff, New York; Richard "Korky" Korkes in Whippany, New Jersey; Bob Metz in Shelbyville, Indiana; and Dave Puhl in Palatine, Illinois. These are just a few of the customizers who continued building new customs in the latter 1950s and well into the 1960s. Many of these later "name-built" cars were seen in magazines and at shows, but I contend that these were really show cars—maybe even "professional customs" if you will—rather than traditional customs. They were

I don't think I'd say Bailon's customs were "quirky," but he definitely had his own style, as seen in the *Mystery Ford* built for Joe Tocchini in 1959. Originally painted candy red over gold, this car has been restored and resides in the Oakland Museum, but for some strange reason it is painted candy red and silver.

I think Richard Del Curto's finned '50 Ford coupe, seen in 1958, is my favorite Bailon custom. It was painted his favorite colors—candy red with gold accents.

built for magazines, for car shows (often to earn promo money for the builder or owner), and to keep the shops open and the builders' names current.

But as far as street customs went, by 1961 Detroit changed its emphasis to nose-up, big-block, four-speed Super Stocks, followed shortly by GTO and 4-4-2 musclecars and then high-performance pony cars. Street customs were nearly forgotten by all but a handful of pom-padoured Anglo "hair boys" and Chicano lowriders during the high performance 1960s. Of course, then came the hippie generation which preferred hand-flower-painted VW Microbuses, followed immediately by the smog-control 1970s with its "gas shortages" that nearly killed auto sports and hobbies altogether. But we'll get to all of this in succeeding chapters.

My favorite shoebox Ford is LeRoy Goulart's lime gold '50 built by Winfield. This second version has canted quad headlights, "scoops(?)" behind the front wheels, and an added lip above the windshield. Interestingly, Goulart's brother Ray did his own custom work on his well-known '50 Oldsmobile.

An excellent example of the later 1950s semi custom style is Ray Kress' lime gold '56 Mercury created in 1958 by Riley's Custom Shop in Chico (75 miles north of Sacramento). It is a definite change from the fat-fender 1940s style, yet still built for style and proportion, not just show points.

Bill Hoffman's super-low '53 Chevy from Portland, Oregon, was used for drag racing as well as cruising and going to shows. This car has frenched headlights, custom taillights, a trimmed toothy grille, and a hardtop roofline.

I present this chopped and sectioned Merc to show that it was built by Darryl Starbird in this candy red, quad-light form as the *Fabula* in the late 1950s.

For our most emphatic example of what trying to win car shows did to custom cars, we present the second form of *Scoopy Doo* by Bailon, as described in the text. We need say no more.

THE SHOW CAR ERA

WHILE THERE MAY

have been smaller gatherings or "shows" for rods and customs at gas stations, car dealers, parking lots, or high schools, usually staged as a fund-raiser for a car club or school group, the first major car show for modified vehicles was the First Annual Hot Rod Exposition and Automotive Equipment Display held at the National Guard Armory in Exposition Park in Los Angeles on January 23, 24, and 25, 1948. The purpose of this show, initiated and presented by the Southern California Timing Association, was to stem, rebut, and "turn around" the Hot Rod Menace image of rodding as presented in the newspapers of the day. The idea was to show to the public highly crafted roadsters and race cars that adhered to stringent safety regulations.

In a Statement of Purpose printed in the official program for that first show, 2 of the 10 points listed were to attract unorganized followers of the sport and induce their voluntary adherence to the self-policing regulations of the SCTA, and to unify and organize the national growth of this activity.

Of the 47 display cars listed in the program, all were roadsters or streamliners, the newest body style listed being a '34 Ford. Another purpose of this show was to allow numerous speed parts manufacturers or services to set up booths to display their wares or capabilities. The program listed 56 such exhibitors.

None of this has much to do with the topic of this chapter, except to point out that, in the beginning, there was no judging, no trophies, and no competition (and apparently no customs, except perhaps for Barris' '41 Buick, which may have been part of his display). However, several key people learned important lessons from this show. First, a hot rod show will attract a huge number of spectators (estimated at 10,000 to 20,000 for the three days), and that translates to a lot of dollars for whoever promotes it. Second, that crowd of spectators means a whole lot of exposure for the parts merchants and other companies who buy booth space. And, at the time of that first show, these merchants had very few other means to reach their target audience.

advertise their products or services. You probably know the result. Petersen hastily founded *Hot Rod* magazine with partner Bob Lindsay and produced the first issue (January 1948) in time to sell it at the hot rod show—although he was relegated to the front steps because the rest of the Associates felt he had two-timed them, and wouldn't let him set up his own booth inside. Of course *Hot Rod* was an immediate and huge success, soon spreading the word (and look) of hot rodding—and to a smaller degree customizing—all across the country.

The early custom car shows were glamorous neither in their displays nor surroundings. This is the first Oakland show, where Jesse Lopez' Barris Ford took a "Special Division" first place. His interior, with rumpled carpets and dirty door jambs, shows these cars were drivers.

Far right

They apparently even let primered cars in. Joe Urritta's chopped and sectioned '41 Ford topless sedan, claimed to be the lowest custom of the time ("The Four-foot Ford"), had a Carson-style top made by Marian Cattles in Sacramento according to Barris.

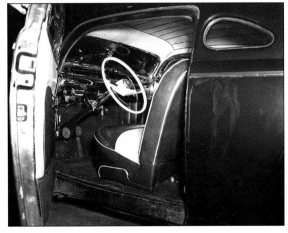

One person on whom none of this was lost was a young Bob Petersen, a member of the public relations group Hollywood Associates, Inc., which the SCTA hired nearly a year before the show to publicize and "direct" it. At least part of Petersen's job was to go around to the various hot rod shops and manufacturers to convince them to buy booth space in the show and ads in the show program. What he quickly realized was (A) there were suddenly a whole lot of these aftermarket hot rod suppliers, and (B) they didn't take much convincing to advertise, because (C) there really was no other outlet in which to

After a second edition of the SCTA Hot Rod show in early 1949 (the program for which had more than 100 advertisers), Petersen decided he could cash in on this car show business, too, and launched Motorama to much fanfare and publicity at the Los Angeles Shrine Convention Hall on November 16–19, 1950. The announcement of this new car show, in the November 1950 issue of *HRM*, stated that its purpose was to raise money to promote the building of a "test timing track" (drag strip) in the Los Angeles area, and that "approximately 40 percent of the net proceeds of Motorama will be employed to get the timing strip

Also at the first Oakland show was Bruce Glenn's Westergard '39 Ford. Show displays consisted of a card with the car's class, number, and the owner's name.

movement under way." There was no mention that there was any connection between Motorama, Inc. and *Hot Rod* or Petersen (though the addresses were the same), and after this announcement, no further mention was ever made of money going toward track development. However, after moving to the Pan Pacific Auditorium, Motorama was a largely successful custom car show for a few years. Now, it has been touted many times (probably by me as well as others) that the Oakland Roadster Show is either the first, or the longest continually running, custom car show. I even incorrectly stated in one article that the first Oakland show was in

1949. Wrong. The first National Roadster Show held at the Exposition Building in Oakland, where the 8-, 8-1/2-, or 9-foot trophy (depending on the report) was given to Bill Niekamp for America's Most Beautiful Roadster, was held January 19 through 22, 1950.

In a booth with some decoration and a display touting Barris Kustoms, at the second Oakland show, Matranga's Merc already has six trophies to brag on. In the smaller photo, which I assume is Oakland 1952, the number of trophies has swelled dramatically.

59

Petersen's Motorama car show debuted at the Shrine auditorium in late 1950. The next year it moved to the streamlined Pan Pacific auditorium, where displays became more elaborate. *Hot Rod* reported that the five-day 1951 show had 102,321 attendees. This '51 Chevy convertible with a '51 Plymouth grille and what appears to be a Gaylord top, is Ken Vertrees' of Anaheim, California, modified by Bill's Body Shop in Fullerton.

Tommy Thornburgh's father owned a Studebaker dealership, so he had Barris customize his '47 Stude convertible, seen surrounded by foliage at Motorama in 1953 or 1954. This car was yellow with an unusual blue Carson top.

Dan Landon's much-chopped '49 Chevy business coupe was another early 1950s Barris creation. It's Motorama show setting might have been inspired by Clifton's Cafeteria in downtown Los Angeles.

However, a small article in the February 1950 issue of *HRM* reports on the "Detroit Show" or "Detroit Hot Rod Show," which was held at Detroit's Convention Hall on January 7–8, 1950. Further, this article states that this exhibition was "the second in two years." It claims an attendance "well over 20,000," and lists Frank Mack's roadster as one of the participants. Who knows who was really first? Either way, it's clear that indoor, multiday, judged hot

rod and custom car shows began sprouting right around 1950.

The Oakland show, reported on by Griff Borgeson in the March 1950 *HRM*, gave awards for Beauty, Construction, Originality, Novelty, and Greatest Contribution to Automotive Industry. Although it was called a roadster show, customs were invited as well, and Barris brought several cars from Southern California. The rods and customs were judged together in a Street Division; it's unclear from Borgeson's report whether there were separate Speedway and Lake Divisions for competition vehicles. For the second Oakland show, it was announced that customs would be judged in their own category, "equal to roadsters."

Borgeson noted that there were exactly 100 cars in the first show, and 40 judges. Of the 43 awards he lists, the Barris Kustom Shop took second (behind the So-Cal streamliner) for Greatest Contribution to Auto Industry, as well as first place, Construction—Street Division; fourth, Originality—Street Division; and Most Magnificent Custom Convertible (as opposed to Most Spectacular, which was a different award). In one of four different classes, each titled simply Special Division, Jesse Lopez' Barris-built '41 Ford took a first. As you can see, from the outset, custom car show classes and judging tended to vary widely from show to show, and could be quite subjective at times.

No one is sure why the SCTA stopped holding its Hot Rod Show after 1949. Tom Medley conjectures that the SCTA was an amateur, volunteer organization, and they weren't in the car show business. Staging a show of that size is a major operation. There is also speculation that

Petersen's Motorama displaced it. A third reason might be that they felt they had accomplished their goal of legitimizing hot rodding.

But 1950 was a big turning point for rodding and customizing for another reason as well. Not only did it see the birth of indoor, judged car shows, but also of weekly, organized drag racing. Both led to more and more cars being taken off the streets, either because they were modified for drag racing to the point that they were no longer street-driveable (rods), or because they were painted, cleaned, chromed, and polished for shows to the point that owners didn't want any dirt, grease, oil, rock chips, or bluing of chromed exhaust from street driving (rods and customs).

Besides the Oakland and Detroit shows already mentioned, *Hot Rod* magazine reported on a show staged at the local Ford dealer's in Modesto by the Century Toppers club (March 1950), one at the Lincoln-Mercury dealer in Whittier (April 1950), and one at the Chevrolet dealer in Sacramento put on by the Thunderbolts club (January 1951). After the formation of the National Hot Rod Association in its offices later in 1951, *Hot Rod*'s focus shifted much more to drag racing than car shows. However, plenty of other car magazines were

In this lineup, the Hirohata Merc has its second paint job, so it must be a 1954 or 1955 Renegades outdoor car show. Also seen are Bugarin's and Bettancourt's Mercs (though that's not Louie with the car—maybe Zupan?) and Bob Dofflow's Ford. What we're demonstrating is that shows were by then all about trophies. The really intriguing part is that Bettancourt's beautiful car didn't get one—maybe because it was too clean and simple?

The first truly radical show car was the *Golden Sahara*. Seen here in its second form, (left), after Bob Metz added his characteristic "split fins" and other updates, it was initially built by Barris (far left) from a new '53 Lincoln Capri that he ran under a hay truck, cutting the top off. Owned by Jim "Street" Skonzakes of Dayton, Ohio, it was finished with greatly extended fenders, built-in Continental kit, bubblelike plexiglass top with gullwings, and a plush interior with full bar, TV, telephone, and other amenities—all in time to make the cover of the May 1953 *Motor Trend*.

Tom Liechty's furry '54 Chevy demonstrates how far show-only machines had come by the latter 1950s. Not only is the chopped top scooped and upholstered, but it has swivel lounge seats, a TV, record player, and phone inside, and it's so low those covered fake side pipes simply sit on the ground, unconnected to the car.

This photo shows that, despite what I say, not all the traditional chopped Mercs and other early customs vanished after 1957. This good-looking, Carson-topped custom Merc was seen in the parking lot at the 1958 NHRA Nats in Oklahoma City, where it drove from California. That's all we know.

springing up at that time to cover the custom car show scene.

The famed Indianapolis Custom Auto Show, held in conjunction with the Memorial Day 500-mile race, also debuted in May 1950. This is the show that Bob Hirohata drove his famous '51 Mercury to, after installing a new Cadillac crate motor and having Gaylord upholster the trunk, in 1953, which he chronicled in the "Kross Kountry in a Kustom" article in the October 1953 *Rod & Custom*. At this show he won a large

trophy for First Place, Custom Car, as voted by the spectators. After Indy, Hirohata and a friend headed north to enter a show somewhere in Michigan. He didn't report how the judging there went. But even by 1953, it was highly unusual to be driving a custom of this quality and

Let's move into the 1960s. This very traditional chopped '50 Merc belonging to Tom Hickel, which looks quite driveable, was presented in a simple display at the 1960 St. Louis car show.

Continued on page 68

Big fins, bullet grille, quad lights, and lots of other custom work are apparent on Anthony Abato's '54 Olds convertible at the 1960 Hartford show. The display includes carpet, trophies, and some sort of furry rope around the edges.

Also presented in a simple display at the 1960 Hartford Autorama, but a much wilder car, is the radically lengthened, chopped, half-topped '54 Ford that made a name for customizer Dick Korkes from New Jersey.

THE FORD CUSTOM CAR CARAVAN

It has often been implied, if not said outright, that Detroit's big three kept a keen eye on what was happening in the hot rod and custom car world. One of the first to acknowledge this interest from Detroit was the Ford Motor Company. First, it invited 18 hot rods and custom cars of Ford origin to the famous Ford Rotunda building in Dearborn in 1955 for a 12-day "Custom Car Show." According to an article in the August 1955 issue of *Car Craft*, Ford was somehow assisted by the Michigan Hot Rod Association in drawing 61,000 spectators to this show. However, one of the real reasons for this show was to present these customized vehicles to the scrutiny of Ford designers and engineers. Other than Tommy Foster's '32 roadster, none of the other rods or customs involved were big name cars, but they were all very nicely done. We know that this show was staged again in 1956, when Hank Rootlieb's hand-crafted '33 roadster and the *Glass Slipper* dragster were flown out from California for it. Beyond that, information is very sketchy. In fact, the Ford Archive has no information on it at all.

Information is likewise hard to find on the Ford Custom Car Caravan. According to an article in Petersen's *Custom Car Yearbook* Number 2, it was conceived early in 1963. Headed by Jacque Passino, manager of Ford's Special Projects Division at the time, the first display consisted only of a 1/25-scale slot car road racetrack surrounded by four stock Ford new cars. But soon the Caravan grew to a large display that included a couple of existing customs, such as Andy DiDia's 427 Ford-powered dream car and Bill Cushenbery's *Silhouette* (converted to Ford small-block power from nailhead Buick), one or two factory prototypes, several

Ford factory race cars, such as Thunderbolt Fairlanes and Shelby Cobra roadsters, and maybe as many as a dozen customized late-model Ford vehicles, built by well-known contemporary customizers to Ford Styling Department designs.

The customizers involved included George Barris (of course), Gene Winfield, the Alexander Brothers, Bill Cushenbery, and Dean Jeffries. Not only did each of them build custom Ford cars included in the display, but they also traveled to the major shows to answer questions and interact with the crowd.

In addition, Ak Miller, who was Ford's "performance advisor" at the time, was on hand at each stop of the Caravan to answer performance-oriented questions from the audience. Plus, there was usually an AMT-sponsored model car contest, with Budd "The Kat" Anderson to oversee it and represent AMT.

Another duty of the "Ford team" was to judge entrants in certain categories, such as competition cars, to present large trophies as "achievement awards" at given shows. Along with the trophy sometimes went a complete 427 engine and, at the end of the year, complete high-performance Ford cars to overall points champions.

To transport this literal caravan across the country (Detroit; Chicago; New York; Washington, D.C.; Florida; Oakland; and Seattle, to name some stops), Ford employed an open tractor-trailer car carrier for the cars as well as a semi and enclosed trailer for the displays and other equipment. Plus there was an "advance man" driving a lettered, mag-wheeled Fairlane from show to show to do advance publicity and make necessary arrangements for the display.

As far as I can determine, the Ford Custom Car Caravan only lasted about three years—1963–1965—if that long. Toward the end, the emphasis was more and more on the performance models, rather than the customs, and the whole thing soon morphed into the Ford Drag Team, usually consisting of a ramp truck and a trailer carrying a couple of cars—much simpler and much more affordable to operate and maintain.

The Ford Custom Car Caravan was an excellent promotional idea, especially for presenting Ford products in an appealing form to young car enthusiasts and buyers. It afforded some lucrative, much-needed work to a handful of professional customizers who were running out of customers. "It was very good money, especially for the time," Dean Jeffries confided to me recently. It wasn't a case of too little, but it was too late. It was musclecar time.

This fastback '63 T-Bird *Italien* was designed by the Ford Styling Department and built in Dearborn.

Continued on next page

My information says this is the same *Styleline* T-Bird built by Barris for AMT in 1961, now updated with a '60 Merc grille, higher peaks in the hood, and lime Metalflake paint.

Upper right
Called the *Allegro*, this small fastback was another Ford Styling Department project done in-house.

It's unknown whether it had a big block or a small block, but this Fairlane with a T-Bolt hood bubble was driven to each show about a week early by the "advance man" to do publicity. Here it is on the starting line at the Fremont drag strip.

Most Caravans included sportier factory stock Fords, as well as Ford-powered Shelby Cobras, this one custom-finished in candy pearl paint.

Upper right
In the early 1960s, Ford was pushing its "compact" models, including pickups. This asymmetrically styled cabover was Gene Winfield's custom contribution to the Caravan.

The *Coyote* was designed by Vince Gardner of Dearborn. An already tiny Falcon convertible, it has been shortened 18 inches, given the asymmetrical treatment, then painted 35 coats of candy lime lacquer by the Alexander Brothers.

This '64 Falcon was significantly modified by Dean Jeffries for the Caravan, and it sure shows a different custom car look than anything that preceded it.

What killed custom cars? Factory musclecars had an awful lot to do with it. They definitely took over the Ford Caravan toward the end, finally morphing into the Ford Drag Team, featuring cars like this Dick Brannan 427 Thunderbolt.

Chuck Atwood's *My Blue Heaven* '59 Ford, sectioned 4 inches by Peatzold Body Shop in Portland, Oregon, has a quiet display at the 1960 show in British Columbia, Canada. But what's that under the car? Angel hair! This car was recently restored and returned to the scene.

Bob Armstrong's '50 Ford convertible from Ontario, Canada, is a traditional 1950s custom that he claimed he drove daily to work (in the winter?), but here it's showing at Buffalo in 1961 surrounded by angel hair, fake grass, and floodlights.

caliber across country to enter—and win—a car show; many of the spectators wouldn't believe it.

Judging, classes, and "rules" for competing in a custom car show varied greatly from show to show, especially before there was any standardization through groups such as the International Show Car Association (ISCA). I have always been amazed by people who build a custom car to win car shows. There's no science to it. It's not empirical. It's not like winning a drag race. It's more like judging Olympic diving. As we've seen, sometimes in the early days rods and customs were lumped together in a "street" class. Sometimes the spectators voted on the winners. As car shows multiplied and progressed, the customs were usually divided into three categories to make judging more fair. Mild or conservative customs were ones that were nosed and decked, maybe had the door handles removed, with custom paint, upholstery, lowering, and accessories like sidepipes or spotlights. The semi custom class had more alterations, such as headlight, taillight, or grille changes, and possibly body modifications, such as scoops or fins. The full or radical custom class was usually for cars with at least one of the following three modifications: chopped top, channeled body, or sectioned body.

Cars were usually judged in categories: paint, upholstery, undercarriage, engine, and so on, often along with some nebulous category such as "overall appearance" or "styling"

Leonard Menard's '59 custom Corvette floats on a sea of angel hair at the 1960 Hartford show. The frenetic paint job was blue, white, and gold. And check out the chromed suspension, tuck-and-roll license cover, and ill-aimed dummy spots. This is not a street driver.

The customizing on James Knight's '60 Chevy convertible, showing in Nashville, Tennessee, in '61, was really quite mild (remember it's only a year old), but tuck-and-roll wheelwells are not street-conducive. However, it must have been his angel hair and tin foil display that garnered the People's Choice trophy.

or some such. There was a maximum number of points for each category, but if your car got 20 out of 25 points for "engine," you were usually not told why (if you received your judging sheet at all). But points for specific modifications, or number of modifications in specific areas, took far greater precedence over general design or aesthetics. Plus, there were points to be gained for such things as "safety equipment," which is why you see gas, oil, and water

cans, flares, and tools in the trunks; as well as for "display." If you didn't have your hood, trunk, and a door open, you usually did not get any points for engine, upholstery, trunk upholstery, or emergency equipment. Then, at many large shows, there was some overall big trophy for Best Custom of the Show, such as the Elegance trophy at Oakland. This award was given, possibly by a group of judges, purely subjectively, with no guidelines or points.

Now, you can clearly see that this system of judging didn't promote subtlety or restraint. More was better. More modifications got more points. If your engine only got 20 out of 25 points, you put more chrome on it, more carburetors, maybe a supercharger to try to get more points at the next show. If you look at custom car magazines as the 1950s and 1960s progressed, you can definitely see the cars getting wilder and wilder, whether it's the same car getting rebuilt annually, or new cars being built to "beat" the older ones. Abetting this was a stipulation made by most show promoters that the same car could not be entered in the same show two years in a row without some major new modifications. The thinking behind this rule was purely selfish on the part of the promoters—they were afraid spectators wouldn't pay to come to the show if they were going to see the same cars as the year before. Everything had to be new and different. Of course, if the cars weren't driven, you could make them

Again, the custom work on Joe Flowers' '56 Chevy, *Venus*, from Columbus, Ohio (seen at the 1961 Buffalo show), was not that extensive, but its detailing and all the little extras like a chromed undercarriage and engine compartment upholstery, won it the 1960–1961 (first ever) ICAS International Championship for most points during the season.

Runner-up to Flowers for the first International Championship was Carl Casper's much more modified '50 Chevy from Flint, Michigan, the *Exotic Empress*. A continually evolving piece for Casper, it is seen here with a bullet grille and wide front bumper at the 1961 Nats show in Indy. How far would you like to ride in those seats?

as wild as you wanted. Didn't get enough points with one blower? Try two.

To give a concrete example of this type of custom car "show win" thinking, I asked Joe Bailon about the '58 Chevrolet Impala named *Scoopy Doo*. He said he built it for a customer named Frank Caraway, who drove it straight from the showroom to Bailon's shop. Caraway told Bailon to make it really wild, so Bailon drew up a design that included 30 scoops in the body. Caraway said "Do it. And paint it pink." So Bailon did. Caraway took the car to Oakland, where Bailon thinks it took first in class, and he toured it to several more area shows that season. But then he brought it back to Bailon's and said, "Recustomize it. I really want to win big." That's when Bailon made the oval tube grilles front and back, molded "visors" to the front and back of

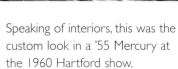

Speaking of interiors, this was the custom look in a '55 Mercury at the 1960 Hartford show.

Angelhairsville! This brand-new '61 T-Bird was customized by Barris for AMT model company Vice President George Toteff. It represents in 1:1 scale how AMT's "Styline" kits could be customized. This is the 1961 Indy Nats show.

Not all 1960s customs, or show cars for that matter, were over-the-top or outlandish. I have always preferred the work of the Alexander Brothers from Detroit. This is a '52 Ford they customized for LeRoy Brooks of Pontiac, Michigan.

This red '58 Ford convertible was done by the Alexander Brothers with a De Soto bumper and quad lights for Tom Biles of Buffalo, New York. Note that the displays are simple and tasteful, like the cars.

My very favorite Alexander Brothers creation is Sy Gregorich's '55 Ford, the *Victorian*. Done for the 1960–1961 season in pearl white and red scallops, it has '53 Stude pans front and rear; '59 Chev front bumper; '55 Olds headlights, and frenched '55 Merc wagon taillights.

Yet another crafty customizer from California of that period was Joe Wilhelm. His silver *Mark I Mist* is certainly hard to identify as a '36 Ford coupe, and it's hard to classify, especially with its sporty recessed wire wheels and sidepipes—but we'll call it a custom.

With bodywork and paint by Bill Hines and lots of custom upholstery by Eddie Martinez, Tats Gotanda's '59 Impala was a semi custom that kept evolving with more and more little tricks (note hooded license, scoops by headlights, chrome fenderwells, rear quarter scoops, underhood upholstery, etc.) to keep winning more show points.

the roof, molded sidepipes from the front wheel openings, recessed the license in the trunk and added a stainless panel, formed tube nerf bars, and painted it candy red and white pearl. This time the car had 40 scoops in it. Caraway entered it in the Oakland show the next year, hoping to win the Elegance trophy for best overall custom, but didn't get it. Which goes to show that you really can't build a custom car expressly to win any given car show.

Interestingly, this radical car was later driven on the street. When asked about the car's fate, Bailon said Caraway crashed it into a bridge one night, crumpling up the left front fender. He brought it to Bailon and said, "I don't want it anymore." So Bailon traded him his own nosed and decked, lowered, candy red '59 Cadillac for it, straight across, and fixed the fender. Bailon had

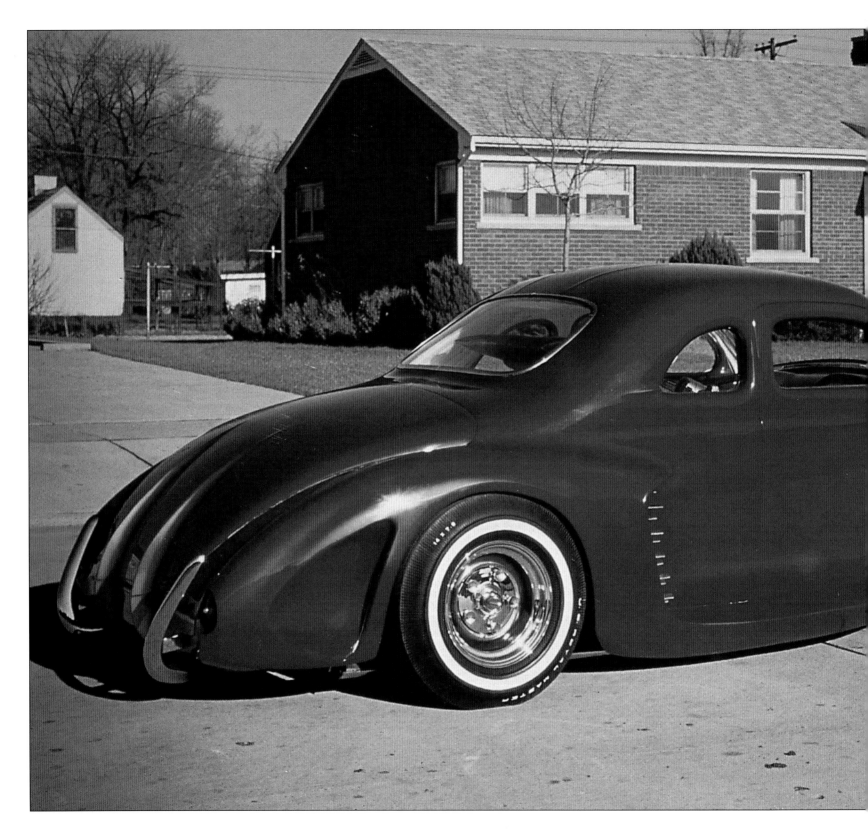

it at a show in San Jose about a year later, and one of the spectators said he had to have it. He had a new "Wide Track" '59 or '60 Pontiac convertible, which he traded, plus cash, for *Scoopy*. Then somebody from Hawaii bought the car and took it over there, where a Chevrolet dealer purchased it and kept it in the showroom for several years. In the late 1960s or early 1970s, someone was driving the car and it got severely wrecked. The insurance company totaled it out, and that was the end of *Scoopy*.

While the *Aztec* was done a couple of years before in the Barris shop by Bill De Carr, the *El Capitola* '57 Chevy was really the last Barris full custom of the show car era—certainly the last by Sam Barris, as he built it at home in Carmichael, California, after leaving the Lynwood shop. Painted white pearl and fuchsia by Junior at Barris' shop for owner Don Fletcher, it won the Elegance Award at Oakland in 1960.

Another stellar customizer of the time with a style all his own was Bill Cushenbery. Again, showing in that 1960–1961 season, his *El Matador* candy red chopped and sectioned '40 coupe was hard to categorize: custom, rod, show car, or driver? It was certainly highly customized, but it's shown here on the street. This car is one more that survives in restored and clone forms.

CHAPTER FOUR

Now this is the era I truly love. The scene is the Los Angeles Winternationals car show, 1962. Take a car, preferably a two-door hardtop or fastback, lower it extremely, add chrome wheels and whitewalls, then smooth it all off and coat it with a luscious paint job in one candy or pearl shade of your favorite popsicle color. Trim the inside in white or color-coordinated tuck-and-roll, and that's all you need—no custom metalwork, no flames, no scallops, no pinstripes. No?

WATSON REIGNS

THE MOVIE *AMERICAN GRAFFITI*

was set in the summer of 1962. One of many things George Lucas got absolutely right in that film was the type-casting of the cars and their drivers. That was the year I started high school, and although I was already steeped in hot rodding by then, if you had asked me which I'd rather have at that moment, a '32 Ford coupe or a '55 Chevy two-door post, I think I would have chosen the '55 Chevy. In my high school parking lot there were two five-window Deuce coupes. There were about a dozen '55 Chevys—jacked up, with the front bumper off, chrome spreader bar between the front frame horns, fender-well headers, American five-spokes in back with Casler cheater slicks, maybe a little bolt-on scoop on the hood, a four-speed if you could afford it, tach on the dash—you probably know the era well. And there wasn't one single custom to be seen in my high school parking lot, let alone the rest of town.

Now, let's look at Lucas' picks. The guy with the hot Deuce coupe was the older guy. The rest were going off to college; he didn't. He worked as a mechanic. He had grease in his hair. He wore blue jeans and a white T-shirt with a cigarette pack rolled in the sleeve. He was a 1950s-type car guy. By 1962 he was suddenly an anachronism. He had the hottest car in town until the new guy showed up with the jacked-up '55 Chevy. This was the hot new trend. Super Stocks and Gassers were ruling the strips. Look at the hot rod magazines. Drag racing and horsepower were in, big time. Customs weren't necessarily out, completely, but they had moved several rungs down the ladder.

Who had the chopped Merc in the movie? The one-percenters of that era. We called them "greasers." This had nothing to do with ethnicity. It had to do with the thick grease in their hair. They were the only ones still wearing jelly rolls, DAs, and long sideburns . . . and those long "car coat" jackets. Their club, the Pharoahs, wasn't exactly a car club—and it certainly wasn't a gang—but it was a social group that was a throw-back, out of sync with what was happening in the first half of the 1960s.

Now check out Richie and his '58 Impala. First off, it's a '58 Impala. You might call it a mild custom. It has red and white tuck-and-roll inside and some custom fogged paint outside, along with '59 Cad bullet taillights. It's nosed and decked and has shaved door handles. But

modified car is almost incidental. It doesn't matter that much anymore, the way it did in the 1940s and 1950s. The Richard Dreyfuss character is similar to Richie—he dresses the same and wears a greaseless haircut—but he drives a Citroen 2CV.

Now here's a second thing to think about. People tend to talk about "the Sixties" as if it were a decade. It's not. It is two very distinct semidecades. In the first half of the 1960s, we had Beach Boys, *Beach Blanket Bingo*, and bleached hair. You could still run your own car at the drags. Rods and custom cars were part of the mix. So were Big Daddy Roth and plastic model

I guess the natural place to start this chapter is with Larry Watson's well-known '50 Chevy, called the *Grapevine*, to point out that it was a typical 1950s semi custom. He showed it, and it was seen in many magazines around 1957, but he also drove it a lot.

Just a year later, Larry bought a brand-new Thunderbird and had the Barris shop shave it and round the corners. Then he painted it a silver pearl, but it was too much. So he masked it off along the body lines and painted a candy burgundy over it, creating the first "panel paint" job. But the point to note is that most of the customizing was done with paint, not metal.

it's got blackwall tires on chromed reversed rims and it sits on a rake. He's got the red mop haircut; he's the high school senior with a letterman sweater; he wears white Levi's or Peggers with button-down Ivy League shirts and penny loafers. If the story were set anywhere near the beach, rather than the northern San Joaquin Valley, he'd be a surfer. The fact that he has a mildly

kits. In the second half of the 1960s, we had Jefferson Airplane and Deep Purple, *Easy Rider*, long hair, love-ins, and hallucinogens. We had Vietnam and the draft. Drag races became "Pro Shows." About the only things on the custom scene were choppers and vans. Bye-bye to Big Daddy, street-driven rods, model cars, and especially custom cars.

After having the Barris shop build him his beautiful (and expensive) chopped Merc just two years earlier, Buddy Alcorn traded it straight across to Dick Jackson for this new, very mildly customized '57 Ford. It is shaved, has bolt-on grille/headlight/taillight mods, subtle scallops/striping, and mild upholstery—and this was enough to make the magazines and shows in 1957.

Where this chapter really begins is with the fin-mobiles of the late 1950s, which we have already discussed. When these wild new cars hit the scene and stole traditional customs' thunder, several of the better-known traditional custom builders, notably George Barris and Dean Jeffries, moved to Hollywood and started building special vehicles for use in movies, and special high-end vehicles for movie stars, rock bands, pro athletes—whoever could pay the bill. Builders in other parts of the country, such as the Alexander Brothers and ClarKaiser in Detroit, found work building prototypes, show cars, or even special drag cars for the auto manufacturers, including the Ford Custom Car Caravan. Others found that they could build "feature cars" that show promoters would pay to put in their shows and tour around the country.

But one guy who really put his mark on the custom car scene—literally—in the late 1950s and early 1960s was Larry Watson. His *Grapevine* '51 Chevy was a traditional mild custom.

Although he was never a member of the Renegades club of Long Beach, he cruised the Clock drive-in on Bellflower Boulevard with them and striped their cars, such as Duane Steck's *Moonglow* '54 Chevy and St. Vasquez' '50 Chevy convertible. To start with, Watson worked out of his parents' driveway, doing pinstriping and a couple of traditional flame jobs. Then in September 1957, he

Other than Sam's *El Capitola*, seen in the last chapter, pretty much the last full-on custom from the Barris shop was Bill Carr's *Aztec*, done largely by Bill "De Carr" Ortega in early 1958. After a lengthy process, this car has finally finished a restoration by Barry Mazza.

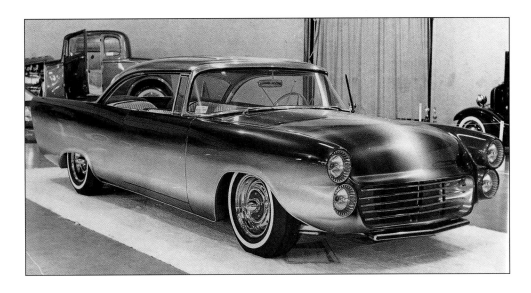

the corners." Watson said that pearls and candies were just coming in then, and he was learning how to paint with them. Most people were shooting pearl over a white base, but he decided he wanted the T-Bird to be a silver pearl—platinum pearl he called it—so he shot six coats of pearl over a fine metallic silver base. "But my problem was, I didn't tint my pearl with what they call transparent mixing black toner. That would eliminate the cloudiness. I got it on pretty even. But the car was too bright. It made it look too large. So I figured 'I'm going to start a new trend.' The

It seems that the indefatigable Gene Winfield just never stopped building breathtaking full customs, but during this period he also started playing—quite successfully—with paint schemes featuring blends of pearls and candies, as seen on the famous *Jade Idol* '56 Merc, built around 1962, or his *Solar Scene* chopped '50 Merc the next year. It's a shame not to show these cars in color.

When Joe Wilhelm built Cliff Inman's '57 Chrysler, he chopped the top, shaved it, made minor taillight and grille changes, and even painted it jet black. It certainly didn't need anything more to knock your socks off. That's Zocchi's Pontiac next to it.

opened his own shop in north Long Beach on Artesia Boulevard, two blocks east of Atlantic. He told me in a recent interview that shortly thereafter he "decided to buy a new car and start a new trend—customizing with paint." So he bought a brand-new '58 Thunderbird and took it to Barris' shop, where Bill Hines and Bill DeCarr "nosed and decked it, shaved the handles, and rounded

Bird, as you know, had the nice panel lines. So I taped it off with 1-3/4-inch tape and shot candy apple burgundy—Nason L113 toner—over that, and came out with the first silver pearl, the first panel paint job, and the first candy burgundy. After it was rubbed out I pinstriped it in gold. It worked good with the burgundy, but not with the silver. So the next day I striped over it in lavender."

Watson started out pinstriping, then sprayed some traditional flames. But soon he was experimenting with various scallops and flame patterns, using creative spray gun fogging techniques.

He also started a trend of customizing late 1950s and early 1960s cars primarily with wild custom paint jobs. "What they did," said Watson, "instead of buying an old car and doing radical custom work, they bought a new car and made payments. After I paneled my T-Bird, it seemed like everybody had to have a panel paint job. Just two solid years of panel painting. A lot of '58 Impalas. I'd use a powder blue pearl with a candy blue, mint pearl with candy green, rose pearl with candy red, banana pearl with candy butterscotch. I'd always paint the car first in a pastel pearl and then come back with a candy."

Watson mentioned one guy who had a full custom '50 Merc with a chopped Carson top and an Olds engine. He traded it straight across for a '58 Impala. When asked where all the old customs like that went, Watson abruptly replied, "Car lots and crushers."

"In late 1957 or 1958," said Watson, "Jack James brought in a brand-new '57 Buick. Downey Buick sponsored him to do the nosing, decking, and black enamel. At the time, for flames, I was just doing the hood, fenders, and into the doors. A front-end flame job like that ran $35. He said, 'No, I want the whole thing flamed. I want the top, I want the trunk, I want a massive flame job.' Now, since he had this big black canvas, I told him I wanted to try a new style of flame job. I wanted to put double licks to it—to stretch it out. He said, 'Whatever you want to do.'"

Watson said the term "Seaweed Flames" came about when Al Lazarus and a buddy painted Lazarus' '55 Chevy black lacquer in the

cruised the front row of Grisinger's drive-in in Long Beach that night," said Watson, "This guy yelled out, 'Look at all the seaweed on that car!' and it became the *Seaweed Wagon*."

I asked Watson to enumerate the various styles of custom painting that he practiced. He said he started with pinstriping, then a couple of flame jobs, then scallops. "In 1957 there was this big show at Hollywood Park. This Jag showed up from up north that was all candy red, by Bailon. Everybody was there—Von Dutch, Junior, Jeffries, Roth, Barris—we were all gathered around this thing. We were doing scallops

When Jack James brought a brand-new '57 Buick to Watson's shop and said he wanted a "massive flame job," Larry decided to try a new, multilick, stretched-out style. It's nosed and decked, and has wheels, pipes, spots, and lowering. But can you imagine cruising this thing down the boulevard—especially when there was nothing else like it?

Al Lazarus shaved and dropped his '55 Bel Air hardtop, added pipes, spots, and a mild grille change, then asked Watson to flame it all over. This car engendered the term "seaweed flames" when someone said it looked like the *Creature from the Black Lagoon*.

backyard and got a couple of flaws in it. He didn't want to repaint it, and asked Watson if he could cover them up. He said, "Sure, we'll do the whole thing." The car had a green and white interior, so Watson used silver metallic with a little black and green toner for the flames, with silver-gold tips, outlined in imitation gold striping. Around that time the movie *Creature from the Black Lagoon* was out, where the creature comes out of the water all draped in seaweed. "When Lazarus

and flames with candy tips, but this was the first full candy job we'd seen. Monday morning I did a friend's '56 Chevy, front and bottom, in candy red over silver metallic. Then I did an MGA in candy purple. Then my T-Bird was my third candy job and first panel."

Watson said his first Metalflake paint job was on Ron Aguirre's Corvette (the *X-Sonic*) in 1960. He painted the car six times as Aguirre kept modifying it. Watson also did his first fade-

Other than Von Dutch himself, about the only other striper laying out flames like Watson at the time was Dean "Kid Jeff" Jeffries, who did this otherwise very mild '50 Ford in 1957.

on it. But then, Watson said, between 1960 and 1966, "I got lazy. I didn't want to do all the masking and striping, so I was doing straight candies with metalflake tops or pearl tops, or pearl bottoms with candy tops to match. I was creating more colors then."

However, during this period he did experiment with a few other designs. He said he was going to shoot some "candy ink" on one job, but it was new acrylic lacquer rather than the old nitrocellulose, and he didn't realize it needed more thinning. When he tested it on a piece of paper, it came out like cobwebs. He was intrigued by the look, so he tried spraying it with no thinner at all. That was even better. He said he did his first cobweb paint design in 1963 or 1964 on a '63 Pontiac.

Sometime later a Binks rep was at the shop and saw him doing this. He said, "How'd you like to do that in a circular pattern?" The next day the rep showed up with a veiling gun and veiling

paint (as used on lampshades and ceramic pieces, like ashtrays, explained Watson). Watson incorporated this into his arsenal of painting tricks.

When he was painting Roth's *Druid Princess* in 1966 (Watson also painted the *Rotar, Road Agent, Mysterion,* and *Orbitron*), he asked the same rep to have Binks make him a double-headed, double cup veiling gun that would swirl two different colors of paint in opposite directions. He still has it.

Sometime in 1966 Watson sold his shop, then on Lakewood Boulevard in Paramount, and went to Mexico pursuing an acting career with his then-wife. Suddenly two other "Watson" custom paint shops sprung up, in Downey and Burbank. When he returned in late 1966, he opened a new shop on Artesia in Lakewood and determined he "had to get his name back on the show circuit." The next big show was at the Los Angeles Sports Arena in April. Watson was painting Doug Carney's '63 Grand Prix for it. He said he was lying in bed one night, thinking: "'I've got to do something different.' Von Dutch

Everything we've seen in this chapter has been from California. What was going on elsewhere? Charles Gibson's '56 Chevy was good for first place in the semi custom class at the 1961 Fort Wayne, Indiana, show. It has Packard taillights, bubble skirts, a roof scoop, and '58 Chevy quad lights. The chrome reversed rims are the only modern element. And it's painted plain white.

At the 1960 St. Louis Autorama, Harold Smith's '59 Impala came all the way from Miami, Florida, to win the semi hardtop class. It's dechromed, has the hood "nostrils" filled, frenched lights, and a tube grille. Most of the customizing is in the interior. The color? Straight black.

had told me about this doily on his bench. He said it was one of the rare times to clean up the shop. This doily had been sitting on his work bench for a long time. When he picked it up, all the overspray left a beautiful design on the bench. So he sprayed clear over it and that was his favorite spot on the bench. I thought, 'I wonder if I can do the whole side of a car like that?' So I went down to a large yardage store in Los Angeles and got this beautiful lace pattern with a Lucky Lager [double X] pattern, not floral, and did his car with it." Some people claim that custom painter Joe Anderson invented lace painting, but an article showing Anderson demonstrating the technique appeared in the March 1968 issue of *Rod & Custom*, nearly a year later.

Watson had 54 cars in the center arena of that 1967 Tridents car show, with a bunch more custom motorcycles on the mezzanine above. This was the pinnacle of his career. But even then, his clientele was pretty much a localized select breed. Watson admitted it

The year here could be as early as 1959, and Watson has plenty of work. The only really customized vehicle in the photo is that chopped '58(?) Ford or Merc, and you can see that Larry is already leaning toward straight candy or candy/pearl combinations that don't require all that masking.

At the same 1961 Indiana show, Bill Stogsdill's near-stock '58 Impala, with scallops so subtle you can barely see them, won Best Stripe and Scallop Paint Award. Change the colors and this could be the American Graffiti Impala.

was regional: "Well yeah. San Fernando Valley was more racers." NHRA historian Greg Sharp went to high school in the early 1960s, in San Pedro, next to Long Beach. As I said, there were no custom cars at that time at my high school in Corona, about 70 miles east of Los Angeles. Greg said his high school parking lot had nothing but mild customs in it. At least in California, in the 1960s, the custom car cult was pretty much localized to the Long Beach, Lynwood, Bell-flower, and Paramount areas, later shifting to Hawthorn and Inglewood.

Corona also had a large Chicano population, and I watched lowriders cruise up and down the streets outside my school windows all through grammar and junior high school. It was strictly a Chicano thing, as far as I knew. When I went to college in the Los Angeles area, I was astounded to see white guys driving lowriders—cars like Buick Rivieras and '65 Chevys, by then with hydraulics and Astro Supreme wheels with nar-

Meanwhile, Watson continued building new, extremely low, custom-painted cars for himself, such as this candy red over white pearl paneled '59 Cad. Those pipes became known as Bellflower tips.

Were the chopped Mercs and other early-style customs completely gone? Almost. But there were diehards here and there like this young, bearded Rod Powell who built this slightly modernized, candy tangerine, chopped '50 Merc and got it in the June 1965 issue of *R&C*, along with Wilhelm's *Mark I Mist*.

row-band whitewall tires. There weren't many of them, and I'd see them mostly in the Hawthorne-Inglewood area, where the aircraft surplus stores (Earl's and Palley's) supplied the hydraulic equipment. The guys who built and drove these cars traded their greasy jellyrolls and long sideburns for tall, combed-back "pompadour" hairdos, while their girlfriends had even taller "beehives." Other than Chicano lowriders, these were the last vestiges of street-driven customs in the latter 1960s/early 1970s.

Watson left the custom car scene in favor of a blossoming TV and movie acting career. He painted or striped numerous luxury or sports cars for actors, actresses, producers, directors, or casting directors to gain entree, and ended up in 141 different shows over a 15-year period, mostly in the 1970s, and usually playing a bad guy of some sort, shooting bullets instead of paint. Of the custom car scene, he said: "Vans and musclecars killed customs in the late 1960s. People just lost interest in customizing cars."

Bob Reisner's twin-engine *Invader* had an aluminum body formed by Don Borth. It won the AMBR in 1967, and tied with Wilhelm's *Wild Dream* in 1968. Amazingly, this car was restored in 2000, and is driving again.

CUSTOM HOT RODS AND BUBBLE TOPS

THIS CHAPTER COVERS

roughly the same time frame as the previous one, except the focus shifts from the street to solely the show floor. Normally I would call the term "custom hot rods," or worse, "custom rods," an oxymoron. Hot rods and custom cars are related by culture, but they are very distinct species. But during the 1960s, as builders competed for show trophies and magazine covers, the line began to blur. Ed Roth's *Outlaw* is unmistakably a hot rod, but what about the *Beatnik Bandit*, the *Mysterion*, and the *Orbitron*? What exactly are they? Well, they're show cars, primarily. While Roth always made his cars fully functional, they were never driven. He didn't enter them in shows to win trophies. First, he'd get them on magazine covers to make them famous. Then he'd put them in shows for two reasons: one, as a feature car to help draw crowds; the promoter might pay a fee for this, or at least give Roth a free booth. Two, to attract customers to Roth's booth, where he would be air-brushing "wierdo" shirts and hawking other items, ranging from decals to hats or helmets. If it also resulted in a deal with a model car company, so much the better, since they paid royalties on every model sold. In other words, Roth's wild cars weren't just show cars, they were commercial show cars. Although no one has ever called them this before, we might think of these "name" feature show cars of the 1960s as professional show cars.

Probably the first of this genre is Dick Peters' Barris-bodied-and-painted *Ala Kart*, which won the big trophy at Oakland in 1958 and 1959. Although it started as a real '29 Model A roadster pickup, every piece of sheet metal on this car was either significantly modified or replaced with hand-formed parts. Its fully chrome-plated and upholstered chassis, plus the candy scallops painted and pinstriped on the undersides of the fenders, fully indicate that this car was not intended to be driven. In fact, in later years when the AMT model company owned it, Budd Anderson tried driving it on the streets of Detroit. The fenders nearly fell off, because of the amount of lead in them, and the engine caught on fire. The *Ala Kart* was followed by Chuck Krikorian's (Peters' brother-in-law) *Emperor* Model A roadster, which not only had a Barris-customized body and hand-formed nose, but also had a completely chromed frame. It won the Oakland show in 1960.

Custom-bodied hot rods go way back, as the Ayala-built Eddie Dye roadster from the early 1950s amply demonstrates. It not only has the handmade nose and hood, but also has the doors welded shut, fenderwells and cowl filled, and a bellypan fairing at the bottom. Several other track-nose jobs would fit in this category, but they're clearly rods, not customs.

The obvious starting place for this chapter is Dick Peters' *Ala Kart*, finished in time to win the big Oakland trophy in 1958 (and 1959). While Peters and Blackie Gegeian did most of the chassis and chrome work, the body was all Barris. You can tell it's a hot rod—in fact, it's a roadster—but the entire body is customized.

This was the same year Roth debuted the *Outlaw*, which resembled a T-bucket roadster, but with a hand-formed body and nose. The *Outlaw* is the only car for which Roth made a four-piece female mold, held together with tool box latches. The idea was that he was going to sell bodies to customers. Ed Fuller, who worked for Roth at the time, once estimated that they made 12 to 15 of these bodies, but I have only seen 2 that were made into cars (and Roth made only the body, not the nose, for sale). The artist Robert Williams, who also worked for Roth, still has this mold today. Roth's more usual method for making his custom

bodies involved laying up a plaster buck (later with a "filler" of insulation called Vermiculite) in the general shape of the body. He would then grind, file, and sand this plaster to the exact shape he wanted, lay fiberglass on top of it, break the plaster out from inside the body once the fiberglass dried, and then grind, file, and sand the fiberglass smooth until it was ready for paint. That is, instead of making a female mold, as is done in most fiberglass forming, he made male molds.

Roth's next, and arguably best, car, the *Beatnik Bandit*, was actually designed in a series of articles in the little pages of *Rod & Custom* magazine by artist/cartoonist Joe Henning. The first version, believe it or not, had a tall "phone booth" Model T-type top. We're not sure who had the idea for the bubble top first, Roth or *X-Sonic* Corvette owner Ron Aguirre, but it was Ron's father, Louie, who devised the method for making the bubbles and also engineered the aircraft surplus hydraulic systems that raised and lowered the top and the front suspension of the *X-Sonic* (generally agreed to be the first custom car with hydraulic suspension). Similar hydraulic systems also steered the *X-Sonic* and the *Beatnik Bandit*.

To make the bubbles, two sheets of 3/4-inch plywood were clamped together with the heated plastic in between. The top piece of plywood was cut out to the shape of the perimeter of the bubble, and the lower sheet had a hole where compressed air could be injected. After making his plywood patterns, Roth said he had Harry First, of First Neon in Los Angeles (which made plastic theater marquees), heat the plastic and blow the bubble. One sidenote is that in every photo you see of Roth in the car, the top is up. He couldn't fit in the car with it down. Both Roth

By 1960, Peters' brother-in-law, Chuck Krikorian, repeated the scenario, building his own chrome chassis, but having Barris custom-build the body. Actually, the body itself is similar to Eddie Dye's, but that nose is from Tomorrowland, not any circle track.

Ed Roth also debuted his fiberglass *Outlaw* in 1960, when it appeared on the January 1960 *Car Craft* cover. It sure rocked the rodding world with this wild new free-form design.

Another early (1960) and ambitious customized rod was show promoter Ray Farhner's pearl blue '32 roadster pickup, later called the *Eclipse*. Restored by Doug Thompson, who originally helped build it, it is part of Jack Walker's custom and clone collection.

The next year Roth helped launch the bubble top era with his incredible *Beatnik Bandit*. It retains a roadster attitude, and its big blown Olds, chrome wheels, and slicks say it's a hot rod—but not like any you've seen before.

Ron Aguirre's '56 Corvette went through numerous custom stages. By 1960 he and his dad completely redid it, adding the plastic bubble. The bubble, the front suspension, and the steering were operated by aircraft hydraulics. Is it a rod? Is it a custom? Well, yes.

and Aguirre had remote controls attached to their cars by plug-in cords, and at shows they could start the engine, raise and lower the top, steer the wheels back and forth and, in Aguirre's case, raise and lower the front suspension. I saw both cars demonstrated this way, several times. In Roth's case (he'd fire it up about every half-hour), it would bring plenty of new potential customers running to his booth. Can you imagine a show promoter allowing this today? Roth also fired up his *Road Agent* this way at shows, but it was his *Rotar* air car that put an end to such demonstrations. At one show, one of the two fans, which were powered by V-twin motorcycle engines, came loose, flew up to the ceiling of the arena, came back down, and injured a spectator.

As I say, the line between rod and custom blurred in this decade. The Aguirre *X-Sonic* certainly had a custom body, but it was based on the performance-oriented Corvette, it had slicks on the back, and it certainly sat on a big rake when the hydraulics were dropped. However, the *X-Sonic*, even in its bubble top version, was street driveable. There were many sightings of it cruising the Riverside area, with Aguirre raising the bubble to chat up girls on the sidewalks.

In the 1940s or 1950s, you could build a '40 Ford coupe as a rod or as a custom. They were very popular either way, and you could readily tell which was which. The custom would be lowered in the back with bubble fender skirts and maybe molded-in fenders (molded to the body). It would have full wheelcovers of some sort. A hot rod '40 Ford would sit on a rake, with no fender skirts, and would have small hubcaps. It would probably be painted some bright color like red or yellow. They'd probably both have tuck-and-roll upholstery and wide whitewall tires, but the rod's would be bigger in back than in front. It's not hard to tell a 1950s rod from a 1950s custom, even if built from the same body style. But how would you categorize a '40 Ford like

And we mustn't leave out Darryl Starbird, who rolled out his first bubble top, the Chrysler Hemi-powered '56 T-Bird *Predicta*, that same year—1960. Although they had hot engines and didn't wear skirts, Starbird's cars were generally more custom than rod.

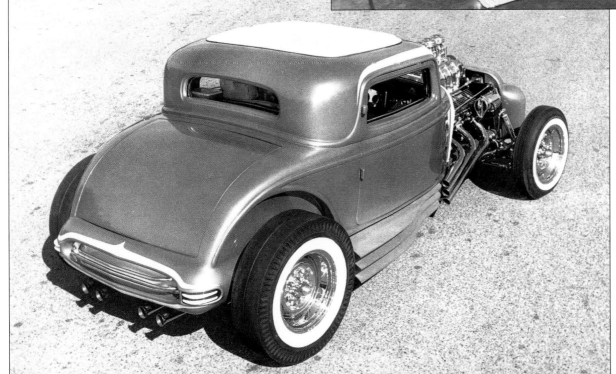

Chili Catallo's blue and white pearl '32 three-window coupe, with a blown Olds engine from his former dragster, was actually built by the Alexander Brothers in Detroit, though they get little credit for it. When he came to Los Angeles for college, he took it to Barris to have the top chopped and the paint retouched. Catallo having recently passed away, his family now has the car and plans to restore it properly.

Another car that went through many iterations was Dave Stuckey's *Little Coffin* '32 sedan, which looked like this by 1963. Although fully custom-bodied, it retains a definite hot rod flavor. It, like several of the cars in this chapter, was made into a 1/25-scale model kit. This car still exists in the Starbird collection, but you'd never recognize it.

Back at the Roth Studios, next from Big Daddy's weird mind came the *Road Agent* in pink pearl by Watson, with a pink-tinged bubble and Corvair power out back. This one was recently restored by Mark Moriarity of Mound, Minnesota.

Bill Cushenbery's *El Matador*? Bob Crespo's sectioned '40 coupe is another example.

When Dean Jeffries built his bubble top beauty, the *Mantaray*, in 1964, he started with a cast-off 1930's Maserati Grand Prix car chassis. Today he wishes he'd restored it instead. But the car, with its asymmetric hand-formed aluminum body, Weber-carbed small-block Ford, and Indy-style mag wheels and tires, is a masterpiece that Jeffries said he "hoped would appeal to sports car enthusiasts, customizers, and rodders." He still has the car today, in pristine condition.

Other examples of these 1960s customized hot rod show cars would include: Ray Fahrner's '32 roadster pickup (1960); Clarence "Chili" Catallo's *Silver Sapphire* '32 coupe (1962); Dave Stuckey's *Little Coffin*

The yellow Roth *Mysterion*, with its two big-block Ford engines and Cycloptic, asymmetric headlight, landed in 1963. We know this one self-destructed while riding in a trailer somewhere between cross-country car shows, and parts were scattered.

Dean Jeffries' *Mantaray* (1964) was much more sophisticated than most gave him credit. It was built on a '30s Maserati Grand Prix chassis, with a Weber-carbureted Ford engine, Indy mag wheels and tires, and a hand-formed aluminum body painted a silver pearl. Remember, Jeffries started out as a pinstriper and shirt painter, but he built this car himself, including metalwork.

Starbird really got that jet-age look in some of his early bubble cars, such as the purple candy *Forcasta* (1962), built on a Corvair chassis. This is actually one of his several double-bubble cars.

'32 sedan (1963); Tex Smith's XR-6 roadster (1963); Bill Cushenbery's *Silhouette* (1963); Carl Casper's twin-blown *Ghost* (1965); Don Lokey's Barris T roadster (1966); Bob Cruces' *Crucifier* roadster (1967); Bob Reisner's twin-engine *Invader* (1967); and Joe Wilhelm's *Wild Dream* (1968). Other than the Roth cars and *X-Sonic* already mentioned, nearly all the rest of the bubble top cars were built by the extremely prolific Bubble Top King, Darryl Starbird at his Star Custom Shop in Wichita, Kansas. The first was the *Predicta* candy blue '56 T-Bird (1960), followed by the purple candy '60 Corvair *Forcasta* (1962), the red '58 Impala *Fantabula* (1962), the three-wheel *Futurista* (1963), and the blue '58 T-Bird *Electra* (1963). The last three were actually double-bubble cars. Starbird still owns the *Predicta* in restored and driveable condition.

Carl Casper's twin-blown, Pontiac-powered (with a Tempest transaxle in the back) *Ghost* won the AMBR in 1965.

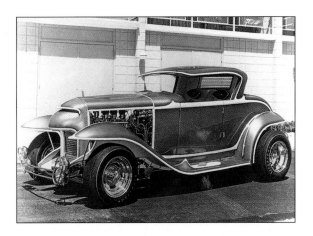

Far left

Joe Wilhelm's purple *Wild Dream*, with an all hand-formed steel body, certainly is, well, wild. He even handmade the wheels. After replacing those front slicks and a few other subtle changes, it tied for the Oakland AMBR trophy in 1968.

Left

We won't name names, but thankfully there were far fewer bad custom hot rods than there were bad customs over the years. It looks like a gennie Deuce roadster sacrificed its life for this, uh, conglomeration, circa 1967.

Joe Cruces, who previously made the cover of *Hot Rod* with a very traditional tall top T coupe, changed gears radically with his completely custom-bodied *Crucifier* roadster.

I called Junior because I knew he did one of the paint jobs on Steve Scott's *Uncertain T*. He said, yes, he did this apricot Metalflake paint. Junior also thinks the *Uncertain T* predated Woods' *Milk Truck*. Just goes to show that history is an uncertain science. No one seems to know what became of this injected Buick-powered show car, but I do have a photo of it running down the San Fernando drag strip.

SILLY SHOW CARS

THE NEXT DEVELOPMENT

on the car show scene was not a pretty sight. Again, we'll be overlapping time periods a bit, and most of these cars are really more rod-based than customs. But in the latter half of the 1960s and into the early 1970s, there really were no customs on the scene other than lowriders.

This era started with Dan Woods' *Milk Truck*, which he built in his parents' garage as a 17-year old the summer after he graduated from Paramount High School in 1964. He said he got the idea from a model car that was built into a similar panel truck, and decided to make it a milk truck because his dad was in the dairy business. Also remember that panel trucks and sedan deliveries were popular at the time because of the surf craze. Woods said he started with a Model A frame that he carted on a wagon behind his bicycle to a muffler shop for welding, and built the body from scrap plywood, nailed together, and then fiberglassed "like a paddle board." Woods was also working in a local body shop at the time, where he painted it pearl white.

Woods got the car finished in time for the 1965 Tridents' car show at the Los Angeles Sports arena, the first of the season, where it won Sweepstakes and landed on the August 1965 cover of *Rod & Custom*. It also led to Woods signing a contract with promoter Gary Canning to put the truck in his string of car shows throughout the West. "I'd get $500 for big shows and $250 for smaller ones," Woods said. This is probably the first instance of a feature car being paid money, especially on a circuit over a full season, on contract. This is a crucial part of this chapter. It also soon became a problem for Woods. "I actually built that car to drive," he said. "We were organizing the Early Times [hot rod club] then, and I wanted to participate, but my car was always in a show." Woods ended up trading the *Milk Truck* to Bob Reisner, future owner of California Show Cars, for a T-bucket.

The *Milk Truck* was significant for several reasons. It had a theme and a name. It had a cartoon quality that attracted and intrigued show goers, especially kids. And it not only helped launch a string of such themed cartoon cars, but it also launched Reisner's and Jay Ohrberg's California Show Cars company, which built (or had built) several such cars and trucked them in big rigs to shows all over the country.

The names of these cars give a good idea of what sort of vehicles they were: the *Outhouse Car*, *Sex Machine* (incorporating a bed and two engines), *Barber Car*, *Bath Tub Car*, *Boothill Express* (with a hearse wagon body), *Turnpike Hauler* (wild tow truck), *Bunk Bed Car*, *Bat Cycle*, *Monster Cycle* (with an Allison V-12 engine), *Martian Spider* (with multitube frame and eight wheels), and *Pink Panther Limousine*, just to mention a few.

When I met Jay Ohrberg in 1974, he was running a business called Mr. Roadster, building and selling parts for fiberglass T-buckets, or "Fad T's" as they were rightly known then, out of a small shop in his backyard in North Hollywood. I had no idea that he was, basically, king of the freak show cars in the previous decade, having been responsible, with Bob Reisner, for creating and promoting many of these vehicles. To be honest, I just didn't pay much attention to these cars, because—especially at the time—I considered them the nadir of car shows and customizing. But when I met

I think Dan Woods' description of why he built his *Milk Truck* kind of sums up this era: He saw a model built like this and decided to build a real one. Most of the cars in this chapter are like full-size model kits. This version of the *Milk Truck* was after Bob Reisner got it and added the purple fogged stripes. Later it even had a supercharger.

Originally painted blue as part of the Ohrberg-Reisner California Show Cars stable, the *Turnpike Hauler* was later repainted candy red and became the *Redd Foxx Wrecker*. Supposedly it now belongs to someone in the Midwest who has a large towing company and who has made it fully operational.

Ohrberg as Mr. Roadster, over in the corner of the driveway was this odd contraption that looked sort of like a small jet engine on a four-wheel gurney. I asked what it was. Ohrberg got this weird, wild look in his eye and said: "That's an iron lung . . . and I'm going to make a car out of it!"

Two other progenitors of this wild show car style, both apparently owner-built, were Steve Scott's wildly leaning, much shortened *Uncertain T,* which appeared on the cover of the November 1965 *Car Craft,* and the *Outhouse,* by Don Bell and Chuck Trantham, which was featured in *Car Craft* in August 1966. Featuring toilets for seats, a plunger for a shifter, a wood body, and a shingled roof, the latter was the one that really launched the "anything ridiculous on wheels" genre of show cars. It was eventually acquired by Reisner and Ohrberg, and became part of the California Show Cars traveling show car circus.

Another customizer who jumped, big-time, into this feature car frenzy was, of course, George Barris, then working out of his Hollywood shop on Riverside Drive. Probably his most famous and clamored-for show cars were the TV cars, beginning with the ever popular *Batmobiles* (there are now seven, we think) and the *Munster Koach* and *Dragula.* These vehicles, along with the curious *Beverly Hillbillies* truck, are still touring custom car shows today, in multiple numbers. Other Barris show machines of this era included the *Surf Woodie,* the *Bathtub Buggy,* and, reflecting the van scene of the 1970s, a well-padded romper room on wheels called the *Love Machine.*

Dean Jeffries also contributed the *Monkeemobile* and the *Green Hornet,* as seen on those respective TV shows.

Now, in the prior decade we had what we might call the pioneering customizers, turning out personalized custom cars, in their own shops, for individual customers, for the most part. In the latter 1960s/early 1970s, most of this kind of custom work stopped. Many of the "name" customizers moved to the Los Angeles area, either briefly or permanently: Gene Winfield, Joe Bailon, Bill Hines, Bill Cushenbery. In fact, it was Cushenbery who was supposed to build the *Batmobile* for the TV series from the Lincoln *Futura* dream car. But, working in sheet metal and lead, he was too slow. The studios needed the car. So it was sent to Barris' Hollywood shop, where it

Many of the silly show cars were just "things bolted together" on whatever chassis was available, as Dick Dean put it. I think this bathtub-mobile was a Barris contribution. Ohrberg-Reisner countered with one that had two bathtubs.

While working at the Barris shop, Dick Dean built the *Vox Mobile* on a Dragmaster kit-T chassis with a small-block Ford engine. It carried real Vox musical instruments that could be demonstrated by performers where the "car" was set up at shows.

The only rationale I can think of for the *Barber Car* is that collectors like old barber chairs. Actually, this was one of the better-designed and constructed vehicles of this genre.

inside, but with multiple (empty) blowers and lots of chromed pipes on the outside.

Plus, with a largely out-of-work talent pool to pull from, and plenty of cheap migrant labor in Southern California, you never knew who actually built the cars. It wasn't George Barris, Bob Reisner, or Jay Ohrberg. They were excellent promoters and instigators, but they now worked in the front office.

One veteran, but largely unheralded, customizer and fabricator who has always been adept at turning out a large quantity of vehicles

was finished up quickly (though still in sheet metal and lead . . . later *Batmobile* "repops" were made from fiberglass). This became the tenor of this show feature car era—build something wild, but do it quickly. That's why many of these wacky feature cars were simply something weird bolted onto a T-bucket chassis. Often the engines (and other mechanicals) had nothing

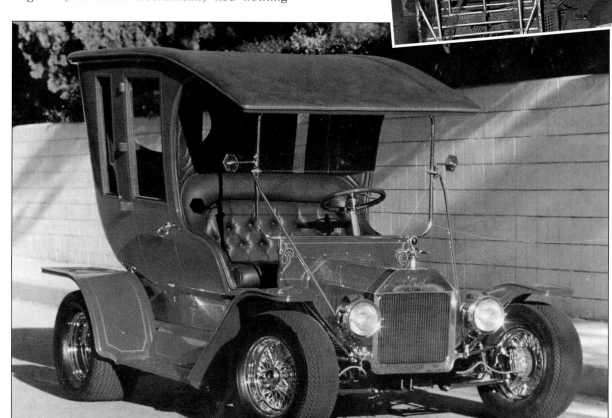

The first time I met Joe Bailon, he was building this exaggerated T out of conduit and sheet metal in the garage behind his house for a customer named Chris Miller. It was finished in candy red and had independent suspension and Tru-Spoke wire wheels. I don't remember seeing it at shows, but I did see it drive to one of the early Lodi, California, rod runs.

in a short amount of time, is Dick Dean. He is one of the guys that Barris and California Show Cars called on repeatedly to turn out all or part of these wild show cars (Barris still hires Dean, in fact). So I visited Dean in his shop in San Jacinto, California, to talk about these times. Here are some excerpts from our conversation:

Dean came out to California from Detroit to work for Barris. He worked in Barris' Atlantic Avenue shop for about six months, then moved to the new Hollywood shop, where he was shop manager for three years. He worked for Barris for five years, in all, in the shop. He said the first Barris project he worked on was the *Air Car*. They built a tube frame fixture, and then had Willie Sutton form the car's aluminum body panels on his English wheel, in his own shop. Next came the *Surf Woodie*, which had a tube space frame and handmade independent front suspension. Then Dean did the *Vox Mobile* for Vox musical instruments.

At the time the Dragmaster Co. in Carlsbad, California, introduced a T-bucket street rod kit with a tube frame, in addition to its well-known dragster chassis. Dean said, "We were getting these chassis from Dragmaster. All I had to do was stick a motor in it, and build something crazy." The Munster coffin (*Dragula*), he mentioned, was a Dragmaster dragster chassis. For the *Vox Mobile* he made giant electric guitars, out of wood, for the sides, and it had an electric organ or piano at the back, that would play. "Tom Daniel was doing a lot of design work for George," Dean said.

After leaving Barris, Dean said he started the *Barber Car* for California Show Cars, and that Joe Bailon finished it up, in CSC's warehouse and shop in Long Beach. He said Bailon also built the *Pink*

What is this thing? Who built it? I think the real question is "Why?" and we don't want to know.

Besides Fad T's, VW dune buggies were another simple platform for these show machines, like this one, which is some sort of "bed-mobile." It's a waste of a good pair of Woodlites.

This El Camino really belongs in the prior chapter. Built by Tom Holden of Detroit around 1963, by 1979 it was apparently on the street sporting a custom trend of the 1970s we're not going to touch—paint tricks that included everything from fish scales and ribbons to freak drops and acetylene smoke.

Panther for CSC in a large warehouse it later had in Hollywood. Incidentally, the first time I met Joe Bailon, in the mid-1970s, he was building an exaggerated, cartoonish T sedan for a customer in the garage behind his house in Hollywood.

Dean also noted that "Ed Newton drew all of these cars. He did the *Wrecker*." Dean said he did three cars for CSC, and mentioned that the double *Bath Tub Car* was done in-house by hired employees. "It was just stuff bolted together, like several of the cars."

Ed Roth's *Druid Princess* fits this era in both time frame and theme. Largely constructed by Jim Jacobs and Dan Woods out of plywood and picture frame decorations, it still exists somewhere in the Midwest.

Referring primarily to California Show Cars and Barris, Dean said: "They started making some money. In those days you could get $2,000 to $3,000 to show a real high-draw piece. That's when the money started rolling in. Bob Larivee [head of Group Promotions] would pay that much to get a specialty car to come in, because it improved the gate. Starbird got to be a pretty good paying promoter, too. He'd pay tow money, put you up in a room, give you a piece of the gate, or a flat fee if you wanted it. But it had to be something special, not some '55 Chevy. It was a wild time, the midrange 1960s. In the 1970s it petered out. Today, half of them won't even pay gas money."

Then Dean summed it up enthusiastically: "It was fun in those days. I mean, I had my own toy factory. Oh boy, we get to build this one? We're going to build what?!"

Bob Larivee Sr., long-time head of Group Promotions, one of the country's oldest and most pro-

lific car show promotion companies, verified those numbers. He said, yes, a top draw car could average $2,500 a show, depending on who paid expenses, and considerably more if it was guaranteed a percentage of the gate. "But we're still paying that today, too, for big-name cars," he added.

Starting out by buying Roth's *Outlaw* and *Beatnik Bandit*, and touring them both through his shows for a couple of years, Larivee ended up commissioning several of these feature cars during the crazy car era. Notable cars include the *Red Baron*, designed by Tom Daniel for Monogram Models and built for Promotions Inc. by Chuck Miller. Before that Larivee had an amazing bubble top, wishbone nose, big-finned creation called the *Stilleto* designed at MPC models and built by Ron Gerstner. Another success was the *Zingers*, a series of miniature rods and customs with full-size supercharged engines, built by Chuck Miller and Steve Tansy.

While some of the pioneering customizers fell by the wayside during this wild, weird era, others, especially in the middle of the country, thrived on it. The Alexander Brothers, Mike and Larry, of Detroit, stuck to tasteful designs, building vehicles for the Ford Custom Car Caravan, and winning the Ridler Award at the Detroit Autorama in 1967 with the *Dodge Deora* pickup, one of their last hurrahs. Larry went on to work for Ford, while Mike went to American Sun Roof. Chuck Miller, also of Detroit, built the aforementioned *Red Baron* and *Zingers* at his Styline Customs shop, as well as the *Fire Truck* C-cab that won the Ridler in 1968. Carl Casper, of Louisville, Kentucky, won the 1964 Oakland AMBR with his twin-blown, fiberglass-bodied *Ghost*. He went on to build numerous themed show cars such as the *Popcorn Wagon, Paddy*

Wagon, and *Beer Wagon*. Steve Tansy, of Tipton, Indiana, was not only a show promoter and drag racer, but he weighed in as a builder with such oddities as the *Pool Hustler* (complete with a full-size, operable pool table), and the *Vending Machine*, with Coke dispenser doors as sides. Jack Kampney, a custom painter from the Detroit area, added the *Mummy Machine*, as well as others, to the mix.

Having first been a custom car builder, and then a big-time show promoter with several major shows throughout middle America each season, Darryl Starbird of Wichita, Kansas, realized that he didn't have to pay big dollars for feature cars—he could build his own. Still a prolific builder, with a large collection of cars and a custom museum, he progressed from the bubble top days to a style uniquely his own, with bodies hand-formed from sheet metal over electrical conduit framing, featuring flared fenders and angular lines. As far as I know, he's never built anything that resembled a popcorn machine or bathtub on wheels, but he does like van or truck-flavored customs.

Finally, the earlier Ed Roth cars were (and are still) definitely in a class all their own. I don't think there will ever be anything else like them. However, I do think the *Druid Princess* fits in the category under current discussion. In the book, *Hot Rods by Ed "Big Daddy" Roth*, Roth said that he initially started building the *Druid Princess* after getting a call from the producer of *The Addams Family* TV show, saying they wanted some sort of vehicle for the family to drive "much like the one Barris had done for *The Munsters*." Working from some Ed Newton design sketches, Roth almost had the car done when the studio called saying the show was canceled. Hitting the show scene in 1967, this was definitely a pivotal vehicle for Roth. He admits in his

book that he had gotten heavily into chopper motorcycles the year before. He left it up to Jim "Jake" Jacobs to tour the car to shows that year, set it up, and sell Roth printed T-shirts and other goodies. Jacobs said the car ran (with a single carburetor inside the blower), and he'd drive it into shows. But one day the engine backfired, and it never ran again. The show promoters wouldn't allow Roth to display his new, 'glass-bodied three-wheel motorcycles in the shows as feature cars, because that wasn't the wholesome, family image they wanted to display. So the next vehicle out of the Roth Studios was what some call the *Bike Truck*, but which Robert Williams tagged *Captain Pepi*. Again designed by Newton, this was a four-wheel "truck" with a single seat cabin on the left, a V-6 with IMSA-style headers on the right, and a classic 1960s Triumph chopper show bike on the back. This was Roth's last gasp to get a custom motorcycle in the shows, and get booth space to sell his wares. But after that it was VW trikes (Roth invented them), *Chopper* magazine with Jacobs as art director, and then bye-bye Big Daddy for nearly a decade.

Darryl Starbird evolved from customizer to car show promoter/producer, but he never got into the goof-ball show car craze. Instead, he has continued to build custom cars in his own unique style, ranging from futuristic bubble tops to more stately fendered cars with side-mount spares as this collection shows. In the back is the Candy blue *Predicta* T-Bird, which he still owns and sometimes drives.

CHAPTER
SEVEN

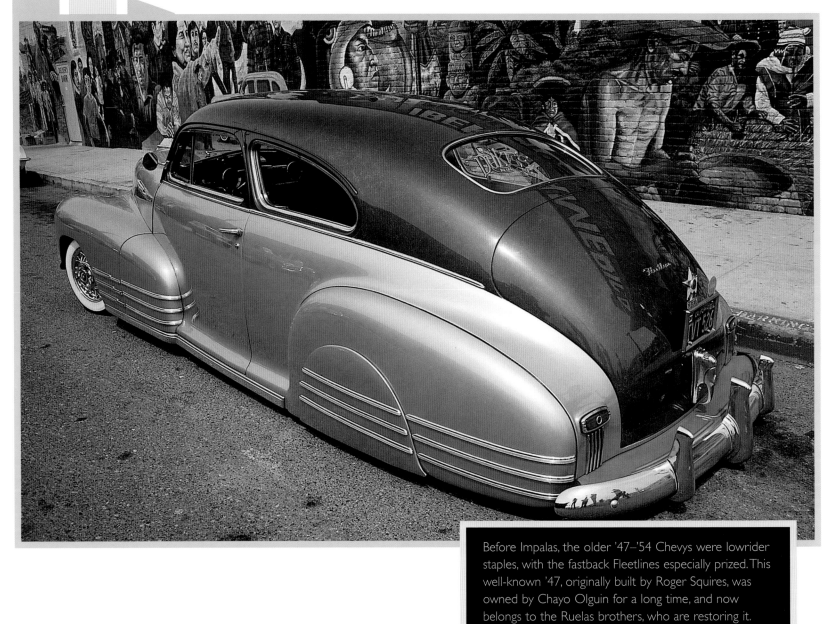

Before Impalas, the older '47–'54 Chevys were lowrider staples, with the fastback Fleetlines especially prized. This well-known '47, originally built by Roger Squires, was owned by Chayo Olguin for a long time, and now belongs to the Ruelas brothers, who are restoring it.

LOWRIDERS

IN THESE MIDDLE

chapters it seems like we're talking more about what aren't custom cars than what are, but that's because there just wasn't much custom car activity during this time. While rods and customs are two distinct types of modified vehicles related by a common culture, custom cars and lowriders are two somewhat similar types of customized cars separated by two distinct cultures. I hope that makes sense to you.

Lowriding certainly grew out of the 1940s and 1950s custom car culture. In fact, it extended it into the latter 1950s and early 1960s. In the early traditional custom era, Chicanos were conspicuous by their presence: the Ayala brothers, Jesse Lopez, Eddie Martinez, Bill "DeCarr" Ortega, Joe Ortiz, Joe Perez, and many others. In fact, early rodding and customizing was very multicultural. But somewhere in the latter 1950s, lowriding veered off as a very separate Chicano culture. The following is a modified (should I say customized?) version of an article I wrote in 1980 for a British rod and custom magazine, explaining lowriders at a point when they suddenly became very popular not only with Chicano participants, but also with the general media:

Seems like everybody is into lowriders. Not too long ago they were the butt of many a snide remark. Now they are intriguing. You may have seen the color spread on them in *Life* magazine [May 1980], or the one in snooty *Road and Track*. Even the *New Yorker* has done a major article on them. The carnival-colored cars with tiny tires that dance up and down on the street have captured our fancy. The play *Zoot Suit*, the movie *Boulevard Nights*, and the TV show *Chico and the Man* have fed this appetite.

In the latter 1950s, when I was in grammar school, I watched the lowriders cruise by. My school was on the "Mexican" side of town. The classrooms had tall windows facing the street—the cruising street—and I spent a lot of time staring out the windows. That's how I learned about lowriders.

Contrary to popular misconception, lowriding is not something new. There are certainly new trends. And there are lots of new lowriders, especially since all the recent publicity. But the culture, the lifestyle, goes back generations. It's a proud heritage.

First let me clarify a couple of points. Lowriding has almost nothing to do with Mexicans. It has developed strictly in the Chicano culture. Chicanos are persons of Mexican heritage born and raised in the United States. Until recently, lowriding was a phenomenon localized in southern and central California. Now it is spreading to other southwestern states like Arizona, New Mexico, and Texas, primarily through the influence of rapidly growing magazines like *Lowrider* and *Q-Vo*. Though lowriding is predominantly a Chicano cult, it has adherents in the black community, as well as a small following among Anglos.

Secondly, and very importantly, a lowrider is not just any car that has been customized and lowered. The early customs of the 1950s, the ones in old magazines, were not lowriders.

Let's go back a bit to see how it came about. In the late 1940s and early 1950s there were hot rods and there were customs. The rods were early Fords built to go fast—they had big tires in the back and were lowered in the front. The customs were the later models, and they were built to look smooth, sleek, and sharp. With lots of lead molding, they were too heavy to go fast, and they were much too nice to race anyway. They were lowered in the back, had fender skirts, and big whitewall tires.

Then, in the early 1960s, rod and custom styles diverged. Show customs became flamboyant creations with candy paint and bubble tops. Hot rods became drag strip diggers. A new breed of street rod/custom emerged, especially in California: later model machines like '55–'60 Chevys, lowered in front, dechromed, with a hot engine and chrome wheels. It was a blend of both rod and custom. Only one group stuck to the earlier custom style—the Chicanos.

They weren't called lowriders back then, except as a term of mild derision by others. Their cars were anachronisms—old Chevys ('49–'54, some older), lowered all the way around, with side pipes, flipper wheel covers, white tuck-and-roll interiors (done in Tijuana), and a Chevy six engine with loud dual exhausts ("twice pipes"). Interestingly, instead of the little steering wheels that became a trademark later, these early lowriders had just the oppo-

site. The driver slunk down low in the seat, his eyes barely peering over the dashboard, looking through the rim of a giant steering wheel. He bobbed up and down as his radically lowered ride bumped over every crack and crevice in the street. The term "lowrider" referred more to the driver than to the car at that time.

A Chicano's car then, as now, was a source of pride. But Chicanos were poor. Early lowriders couldn't afford custom wheels, lots of chrome, or lavish paint. Most of the cars were primered, or had primer spots where chrome had been removed or dents had been fixed. Many simply had highly waxed original paint jobs, including primer spots and places where the paint was rubbed through.

There weren't many car clubs. It was more like all lowriders belonged, by heritage and by elimination, to one big unnamed club united by race, poverty, and pride. Later they would call this brotherhood "gente" or "La Raza."

Cruising was the life ("la vida"). While other kids were revving their engines and burning rubber at every stop light, the lowrider was going low and going slow, shifting from first into third and cruising down the street at a snail's pace. How this driving style got started is unknown, but presumably the lowness of the cars and the lack of spring travel had a lot to do with it. But it was also a statement. A cruiser was saying, "Hey, look at me and my ride. Take a good long look. I'm proud of it." At the same time he was showing that he was different from the kids with their fast cars.

A NEW LOOK DEVELOPS

In many ways lowriding has changed very little over the past 20 or 30 years [and that continues to be largely true today]. In other ways it has changed a lot. The current [1980] lowrider look evolved in the late 1960s, when the '63–'64 Impala became *the* car to have. Longer, wider late models had a sleeker look when lowered. They had more class. Custom wheels—deep five-spoke Supremes—became standard, fitted with little VW-size 5.20x15 narrow whitewalls to get the car as low as possible. Primer spots were giving way to bright paint jobs; metalflake was popular. The late 1960s was a period of social change. Chicanos were getting better jobs, making more money.

About this same time, a few lowriders began experimenting with hydraulic lifts. The components came from aircraft surplus stores like Earl's in Lawndale and Palley's in Los Nietos. The pumps, cylinders, valves, and other components were originally designed to operate landing gear or wing flaps on airplanes. To adapt them to an automobile chassis took a considerable amount of backyard engineering. In the beginning the owner had to do the installation himself. Soon the surplus stores were selling the components in kits (called "trays"). Since they operated on 24 volts (standard for aircraft), extra batteries, wired in series, were mounted in the trunk to run the system, and had to be frequently recharged. Like early hot rodders who stole hubcaps, some lowriders became infamous as battery thieves.

Since aircraft components are expensive and not readily available, lowriders soon discovered that a compact, 12-volt hydraulic pump used to operate tailgate lifts on delivery trucks could easily be adapted to their suspension lifts. Not only that, but these pumps could be quickly unbolted and pirated from unguarded parked trucks.

In essence, hydraulic lifts are one of the most practical inventions ever applied to custom cars. Early radically lowered customs dragged their tails, scraped the ground, and could barely maneuver in and out of driveways. Cars lowered this much were also illegal. A readily adjustable suspension, allowing the car to be raised or lowered at the flick of a switch, was an obvious answer, but one that took some pioneering ingenuity to develop. Ironically, the police have frowned on hydraulics, as well, for little reason.

However, once the system was invented, its novelty soon overshadowed its practicality. A fully lifted lowrider (one with hydraulics at all four wheels) could literally be made to dance down the street. If the front or rear was suddenly dropped as the car sped down a street at night, sparks would shower from underneath as the frame scraped the pavement. Some attached steel—or magnesium—skid plates to the chassis for this show. And when 24 or more volts were hooked to the 12-volt tailgate pumps, lowriders found that the extra jolt to the hydraulics would raise the car so fast it would actually hop off the ground. Suddenly a new, strange, and somewhat questionable automotive sport was created—car hopping.

A hopping contest, unquestionably, is a sight to behold. Impromptu matches are often staged right on the street. Two passing lowriders will stop, nose to nose, and the drivers begin flicking the front hydraulic switches so that the cars begin to bounce up, down, up, down, until the front wheels are bounding 2 to 3 feet off the ground. Organized hopping contests, a major attraction at most lowrider "happenings," test one car at a time. A yardstick measures the highest distance cleared between the tire and the pavement. For these contests, many owners attach remote switches to the hydraulics so they can operate them from outside the car. As might be expected, special "hoppers" have been built, with a trunkload of batteries for extra juice and ballast, and a raised rear axle for clearance. The record hop [in 1980] exceeds 120 inches.

THE STATE OF THE ART, CIRCA 1980

Just as lowriders clung to the styles and traditions of customs of the 1950s, they have long been linked with the evils attributed to hoodlum carboys of that period—partially through their own fault. As one old-timer explained to me, "Lowriding appeals to bad dudes, whether they're black, white, or Chicano." But lowriders are now organizing, primarily through close-knit car clubs, to dispel the pachuco gang image.

These days car clubs and barrio gangs are no longer synonymous. Clubs are growing and gaining in prestige. Getting into one can be as difficult as joining the L.A. Roadsters. Not only must a prospective member have a sharp, first-quality ride, but he must present a good image. This is not to say that some friction between clubs, or between club members and "cholos" does not persist. Police harrassment of lowriders is still amazingly rife. But many clubs are working diligently to earn a good name for themselves and for all lowriders. They enter parades, hold benefit shows, do good works for local communities—things hot rod clubs were doing a generation before to clean up their own image.

The quality of the cars has increased tremendously, too. Lowrider clubs, especially the Imperials of Los Angeles, began entering major car shows in the early 1970s. This was the era of '63–'66 Chevys, Metalflake paint, chain steering wheels, twisted bar grilles, and lavish velvet interiors. Some showgoers considered them gaudy, but these show cars were immaculately detailed, often with fully chromed and painted undercarriages.

These show cars inspired others, and soon more clubs were entering. Interclub rivalry that once precipitated fighting in the street turned to a determined rivalry between clubs to build the best cars, and to win the biggest trophies. It was a matter of pride.

Today lowriding has progressed to a point closely resembling the state of street rodding here [as of 1980]. Styles are refined. Taste has improved with subtlety. Amazing sums of money are being invested in these cars. And what were once strictly show cars are now being driven proudly on the street.

As in street rodding, there is a strong resurgence of nostalgia. For lowriders, this means a resurrection of the older cars—'37–'54 Chevys. These receive the trappings of 1950s customs: fender skirts, side pipes, spotlights, and so on. But chrome that was once molded off is left intact and added to with all the accessories offered when the car was new: extra bumper guards, fog lights, headlight shades, etc. These "resto-lowriders" [now called "bombs"] usually feature original type paint and genuine mohair or early-style white tuck-and-roll upholstery. Most are fully lifted and wear the standard wheel/tire combination of Tru-Spokes and 5.20x15 or 5.20x14 whitewalls.

Late models still predominate, however. Until recently big, classy, sleek GM products were the favorites—Monte Carlos, Buick Rivieras, '75–'76 Caprices or Impalas. But when GM switched to the boxy European look, for the first time lowriders turned to Ford products with their long hoods, stately grilles, and low rooflines— LTD's, Thunderbirds, and even Lincoln Continentals.

The first order of modification, after wheels and lifts, is a full custom paint job. Beautiful hues of candy colors are the order—deep candy reds, lavenders, sapphire blues, lime greens. The paint jobs are exquisite and flawless. Then they are trimmed with airbrushed murals, often depicting Aztec or street cruising scenes, plus pinstriping in a new curlyque style. Red velvet, chandeliers, and mirror glass have given way to more subtle interiors in mohair or color-coordinated fabrics, and even small steering wheels seem to be falling out of favor.

Besides the mandatory Tru-Spokes and little tires, the real essential for a lowrider is a full set of hydraulics. No longer does a car builder have to sneak around truck yards at night to get his components. Several hydraulic outfitters offer complete packages of pumps, valves, cylinders, solenoids, switches, and braided stainless steel hoses for $350–$400 [in 1980]. Or, if the customer wants the entire system installed on the spot, most shops will send him hopping for about $700. That's pretty cheap considering the amount of labor involved to install a four-wheel system. It requires a considerable amount of chassis reworking, plus spring cutting, hose plumbing, and electrical hook-up.

In components, the art of hydraulic suspensions has progressed considerably. Rather than a mis-match of ex-aircraft parts, today's shops offer a variety of integrated components designed to work with the standard tailgate pumps. The nomenclature is as esoteric as Chicano slang: Big Reds, Montes, or D&H cylinders, gold bottom or Waterman dumps, slow down valves, donuts, hats, cups, step downs, and so on. Installations in most cars are quite sanitary, with meticulous wiring, plumbing, and hose routing. Many of the parts are often chrome or brass plated.

However, the engineering of hydraulic systems—fitting the lift cylinders to the suspension—has changed little, and this should be the next major area of progress. In most cases, coil springs are cut down to about four turns, and then the hydraulic cylinder is fitted between the top of the spring and the upper spring mount. Many times the shock absorber, which was inside the coil spring, is simply eliminated—not a wise practice. I predict that in the future we will be seeing such things as torsion bar suspensions with hydraulic cylinders attached to the fixed end of the torsion bars, or possibly laterally opposed cylinders working on the suspension by means of bellcranks. Numerous possibilities remain to be explored.

So what is a lowrider? I once mentioned to the owner of a '48 Chevy Fleetmaster four-door that I had one just like it. "Is it a lowrider?" he asked. I said not exactly. "Is it lowered?" he asked next. I said it was, but it was lower in the front than in the back. "Does it have a six with twice pipes?" I said yes, but it's really more of a hot rod than a lowrider. "What kind of wheels has it got?" was his last question. When I said, "Tru-Spokes," he assured me, "Then it's a lowrider!" I felt honored.

But my '48 Chevy isn't a lowrider. If it had 5.20 whitewall tires, a sun visor, fender skirts, and was lowered considerably more in the back, maybe it would qualify. Yet I feel honored at how readily one lowrider is willing to accept and appreciate a car like mine— just as I appreciate his. More and more, especially here in California, we are seeing street rodders and lowriders at the same functions, swapping parts and digging on each others' cars. That's considerable progress on everybody's part, and certainly no lessening of the lowriders' pride.

When we did the first chopped Merc issue of *Street Rodder* magazine back in November 1974, the only chopped Merc we could find was actually a lowrider, built and owned by Charlie Lopez.

In the late 1970s, when GM cars started getting boxier, some lowriders switched their allegiance to the longer-hooded, more elegant Ford products for the first time. You have to admit that this lowered Mark V has a lot more class than, say, a '78 Impala or Caprice.

Some of the finest bombs come out of Joe Epstein's shop on Whittier Boulevard in Montebello. This is Epstein's well-accessorized '39 Chevy delivery riding on straight-laced spoke wheels.

For the last couple of decades the '63–'64 Impalas have been to lowriding what the '49–'51 Merc is to customizing. This '64 wears candy magenta with multicandy graphics.

When it comes to lowriders, bigger is better. Impalas will always be popular, and murals are still very much in vogue.

We did mention big, right? These '70s Chevy Caprice Classics were about as big as they came. Note that multicolor paint or murals are not necessary, but a quality paint job such as this candy red, is. Also, Tru-Spoke wires seen here have given way to straight-laced, many-spoked Daytons, often with gold plating.

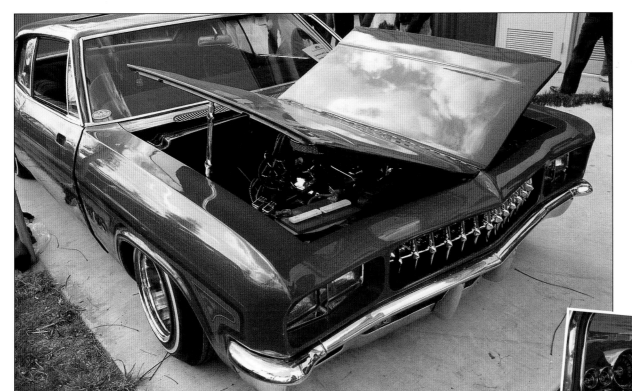

This Chevy has suicide doors as well as a butterfly hood. But also note the custom headlights and grille. Many lowriders incorporate custom body modifications to some degree.

Since that article was written, at the peak of lowriding's popularity, there has been little progress. In the August 1992 issue of *Rod & Custom* magazine, I included a feature on "bomb" lowriders, showed some street rods and customs with innovative hydraulic suspensions, and did a technical article on hydraulic components and systems, with diagrams of several improved ways to install them. Since then, street rods and today's latter-day customs have largely embraced adjustable air bag suspensions, and lowriders tend to install hydraulics the way they always have, albeit with custom components made by companies like Red's Hydraulics and Orlies, rather than truck lift-gate pumps.

In terms of vehicles, the first big new trend in lowriders was minitrucks, which led to the bizarre craze of bed dancing. Using hydraulics, scissors jacks, and other componentry, the owner of such a truck could raise and lower the pickup bed, move it from side to side, and even spin it around like a propeller, in time to loud music, to the delight of a crowd. This was primarily done at big lowrider outdoor shows, in competition. The same goes for hopping contests, which are rarely seen on the street anymore.

The next phase was Euros, or the acceptance of small foreign or U.S. vehicles as lowriders. But they are still modified in the traditional lowrider way: wire wheels, hydraulics, wild custom paint, murals, crushed velvet upholstery, and so on. Another new category, which also competes at lowrider events, is "boomers" fitted with mega-watt stereo systems and lots of big speakers.

Shaggy carpet, crushed velvet, and little chromed chain steering wheels became nearly cliché lowrider interior staples for a long time. Today, some are getting away from it, though it's surprising how many aren't. Plush upholstery and lots of interior chrome are lowrider musts.

It was probably inevitable that hydraulics would be turned into playthings, but it is impressive to see a lowrider "hop." Serious hoppers use an extension cord to control the hydraulics from a distance. The owner of this '58 Impala is flicking the switches in the interior.

The older Chevys, such as this candy red and silver metalflake '52 hardtop, have always been a part of the lowrider mix, and accessories like visors, continental kits, and bumper overrides are cool.

This '38 Chevy two-door sedan from the 1970s is tame by today's standards.

Tru-Spoke wire wheels are gone, replaced by straight-laced, many-spoked Daytons or Crowns, sometimes gold-plated. In fact, today's lowriders often have a considerable amount of gold-plating in place of chrome. But there's plenty of chrome, too, many times coating every removable part from the engine and undercarriage. And while the current lowrider magazines are filled with ads for large-diameter billet aluminum wheels in a dizzying array of patterns, the cars featured and seen at shows tend almost exclusively to wear deep-dish, straight-laced, chrome or partially gold plated wire wheels with small-diameter, small-band whitewall tires.

Bombs—predominantly Chevys of the late 1930s and 1940s—are more popular than ever, with as many period accessories added as possible.

They usually have original-style mohair upholstery, and, again, as many interior accessories as can be found. They can either be lifted with wire wheels and little whitewalls, or on lowering blocks with stock wheels and hubcaps, 1950s-style flipper wheelcovers, or prized rare "artillery" wheels, with wide "gangster" whitewalls. The engines are invariably original sixes, either impeccably restored, or fully chromed. Some clubs, such as the venerable Dukes of Los Angeles (and several other chapters), the Viejitos, and the Old Memories, accept only '54 and earlier bombs as member cars.

I have seen a few breakaway, more high-tech lowriders recently, fitted with such innovations as natural-toned leather interiors, billet aluminum wheels and steering wheels, smoothed and shaved bodies (such as 1960s Buick Rivieras), with single-color pearl paint jobs. But for the most part, as of the turn of the century, lowriders are sticking to the traditional accessorized bomb look, or the traditional multipanel or mural paint, velvet interior, tons of chrome, and wire wheel/little whitewall look. The investment and detailing in these cars is nearly incredible. The sad part is that, so much like street rodding in the same period, these cars are now being trailered to shows to compete for trophies, rather than being driven on the street.

LOWRIDER SLANG

A todo madre (A.T.M.)	Literally, "the whole mother"; it means far out, right on, exactly right
Aztlan	"Aztec land"; it now means California or the Southwest
Bad	Good
Bajito	Low (as in lowered car)
Bajito Y Suavecito	Low and slow
Barrio (varrio)	A poor Chicano neighborhood or ghetto
Califas	California; names of cities and barrios are also cryptically shortened
Carnales	Brothers, as in a brotherhood
Carrucha, rucha	Literally "wheelbarrow"; a slang term for "car"
Cholo	Literally "halfbreed"; it connotes a bad dude, a pachuco
Chuco	Short for pachuco; same as cholo
Con Safos, C/S	Written under a graffito, it means "back on you," or "same to you" to anyone who defaces it
Ese; esa	Literally "that" or "that one"; often used as a punctuation, like "yeah!"; also denotes a guy or dude, chick or girl
Firme	Literally "firm"; tough, sharp, A.T.M.
Flaco	"Skinny"; a typical Chicano nickname
Gente	"The people"
Homeboy, Homie	A gang member from a specific barrio; today it also refers to an accepted member of the group
La Onda	Literally, a wave or a ripple; an event, something that makes something else happen; a trend; sometimes "the world"
La Placa	The police
La Raza	"The race"; Chicanos, gente
La Vida	"The life"; often la vida loca: the crazy life or the gang life
Puro Class	"Pure class"; ultimate style
Q-vo	Short for "que onda"; same as former "que pasa": what's happening? How's it going?
Ranfla	Car
Sabor	"Taste"; as in puro class
Suave, Suavecito	Cool, suave, with style
Vato	From "gato"—cat; a dude, guy

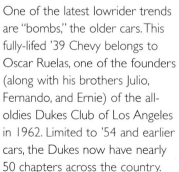

One of the latest lowrider trends are "bombs," the older cars. This fully-lifed '39 Chevy belongs to Oscar Ruelas, one of the founders (along with his brothers Julio, Fernando, and Ernie) of the all-oldies Dukes Club of Los Angeles in 1962. Limited to '54 and earlier cars, the Dukes now have nearly 50 chapters across the country.

Above
Engines in the bombs are usually chromed and polished stock sixes, or fully restored ones in the right colors with gennie decals and accessories.

CHAPTER
EIGHT

With gold scallops over burgundy, white tuck-and-roll, and a '54 Pontiac grille, Kurt Schroeder's '51 Ford from St. Charles, Missouri, is one sharp shoebox.

THE CUSTOM CAR REVIVAL

THERE HAS LONG BEEN

a debate, especially among journalists, whether the media can instigate trends, or whether it merely reports on them once they happen. I tend to think the latter is usually true. However, by the early 1970s the custom car scene was all but dead, especially as far as the street was concerned. I had joined the staff of *Street Rodder* magazine in late 1973, being first listed as associate editor in the January 1974 issue. By the November 1974 issue I was listed as technical editor, though I was essentially doing the whole magazine, with the help of part-time free-lancer Frank Oddo. Jim Clark, listed as editor, and R.K. Smith, listed as managing editor, were by then running the entire McMullen publishing company (then known as TRM Publications). I really can't remember the sequence of events, but—although it was not labeled such—that November 1974 issue (the first to cost one dollar) was the first "chopped Merc issue" of *Street Rodder*. It was centered around some pen-and-ink sketches by then-Standard Brands paint store clerk Jerry Weesner of four famous chopped Mercs of days past (Louie Bettancourt's, Bob Hirohata's, Rod Powell's, and Gene Winfield's *Solar Scene*), along with drawings showing, in just four pages, how to chop a Merc.

The only chopped Merc we could find to feature was actually a lowrider. I started following its construction in Charlie Lopez' garage, and we featured it in finished Metalflake and scalloped form on the cover and three pages inside. We were so desperate to find any other chopped Mercs, I went up to Universal Studios and photographed the horrible, made-in-a-couple-of-days *American Graffiti* Merc, which was on display there. In the readers' cars pages (called Early Iron) we showed three Mercs, but none was chopped or customized. That was it. There were no true customs to be found.

In the October 1975 issue I featured Harry Bradley's *La Jolla* full-custom '51 Chevy, but it was a relic from the 1950s that he brought out of mothballs for a short period of time. (It has recently been sold to Jack Walker, who has restored it.) For the April 1976 issue, I found and featured a Carson-topped '47 Ford with a '46 Olds grille and Plymouth ripple bumpers, originally built in 1956, and rebuilt by Bill Thompson of Grand Junction, Colorado. Then, in the October 1976 issue we featured Pete Chapouris' beautiful, mild custom '50 Chevy

hardtop, but it wasn't on the scene long. By February of 1977 we had Roth on a trike on the cover, and the next month we featured the new craze—minitrucks.

But by August of that year, when we did the first announced "Special Merc Issue," we actually had a new, very traditional chopped '50/'51 Merc (belonging to high schooler Steve Gonzalez, chopped and finished in lead by his father, Blas) to feature on the cover. Inside the book, I was able to come up with 14 more chopped '49–'51 Mercs, combing every source I could find across

The cover car for the 1977 chopped Merc issue of *Street Rodder* was high schooler Steve Gonzales' '51 Merc, chopped and customized in lead by his father, Blas. Other than the '50 rear window, '54 Chevy grille, GM persimmon paint, and '55 Chevy side trim, it's based loosely on the Hirohata Merc.

Featured in that 1977 chopped Merc issue were these two '50 Mercs built and owned by the late Miles Masa from Downers Grove, Illinois. For the convertible, he made a fiberglass mold for the Carson-style top. The four-inch chopped coupe has a Chrysler Hemi engine.

the country. These included three unfinished ones in a club called the Mercs of SoCal; Curly Tremaine's candy tangerine '50; Bob Larivee's *Green Flame* (inspired by a Robert Williams poster); Fred Steele's yellow *Kross Kountry Kustom*; and two, a coupe and a convertible, by the late Chicago-area customizer Miles Masa. In a last-minute two-column addition to that issue, we showed a chopped '51 four-door by Frank De Rosa, an early version of Richard Zocchi's *Cool 50*, and a white pearl '51 owned by "John Augustine" (John D'Agostino). Besides coverage of a Mercs of SoCal meet, that issue also included two pages of design sketches for '49–'51 Mercs by Harry Bradley, and an interview with Bob Hirohata by Greg Sharp, including photos of several of the classic custom Mercs of the 1950s.

But I hope it might have been the editorial in that issue that actually had more impact on the revival of 1950s-style custom cars. In it, I asked why not bring 1950s mild customs back into the

mix? The raw material was plentiful and affordable (unlike Deuce coupes or roadsters at the time), and they could easily be built at home by any competent rodder (unlike a chopped Merc). To quote from that editorial:

Richard Zocchi was one of the first to re enter the custom scene in the mid-1970s with his *Cool 50* Merc chopped at Rod Powell's shop and first painted all candy red. Later he added Riviera side chrome and painted the lower body silver, as seen on the July 1978 *Street Rodder* cover.

Speaking of post–1948 customs . . . what ever became of them? The Mercs are really making a comeback—but what ever happened to all those other street-driven "mild customs" that were so prevalent in the late 1950s and early 1960s? I don't know about you, but I have always liked these cars much better than the radical customs that you would always see in the shows and on the magazine covers. The cars I am talking about are ones like '55–'57 Fords, '55–'56 Mercurys, '55–'56 Buicks, '58 Impalas, '59–'60 Chevys, '60 Pontiacs. And by mild customs I mean smooth, clean, low street machines with frenched head and taillights, tube grilles, perhaps a frenched aerial or a louvered hood, definitely with all excess chrome and handles removed. Paint would be simple and straightforward—usually a solid metallic or

candy color like pagan gold or lime green or Titian red or burgundy. Some of the builders liked scallops or flames—but I liked the straight colors best. And of course the interiors were done up in "coordinated" tuck-and-roll, with lots of white for contrast.

Perhaps my taste is peculiar. But it really surprises me that this "street custom" trend, which was going so strong before the muscle cars hit the scene, has apparently completely faded into oblivion. Where did all those '58 and '59 Impalas go—the ones that were customized as soon as the owners got them home from the new car dealers? What about the '57 Fords with pearl paint and chrome tube grilles and pickup headlight rims and bullet taillights? There used to be dozens of them driving the streets when I was in high school.

The first KKOA Leadsled Spectacular was held in Wichita, Kansas, in 1981. On the left is customizer Eldon Titus' *Crimson Skull* Buick. Eldon is the brother of KKOA founder Jerry Titus.

One of the standout cars at the first KKOA meet was Rick Schnell's '50 Merc convertible from Minnesota. Although it was flathead powered and traditional in styling, it was an all-new car.

Center Image
Wayne Jones of Indianapolis bought this '50 Ford as his first car in 1956. He installed a Chrysler Hemi engine a year later and started minor custom bodywork. He finally chopped the top and painted the candy blue flames in 1980.

I don't think this one editorial revived the custom car scene, but I think that encouraging, pushing, and featuring 1950s customs in the magazine certainly helped (as did Dave Bell's depiction of traditional customs in his "Henry HiRise" cartoons and column heads for years in *Street Rodder*).

It should be noted that there were no other magazines featuring custom cars at this time. In the early 1970s, before it went away in May 1974, *Rod & Custom* was pushing its new invention—street rodding, the Street Rod Nationals, and the NSRA. *Car Craft* turned into a drag racing magazine. So did *Hot Rod* for the first two or three years of the 1970s, then it caromed between drag racing and vans, Vettes, dune buggies, new cars, pickups, ski boats—you name it. During Terry Cook's zany stint as editor

Local custom legend Darryl Starbird was cruising the Wichita grounds in this candy red, fully customized '59 El Camino shop truck.

Doug Reed's scalloped '49 Olds fastback, on a big rake with Fiesta flippers and a tri-carb 372 under the hood, is exactly the kind of car my friends drove in high school in the early 1960s. We wouldn't call it a custom, just a hot car. A Wichita resident, Reed had it at the 1st KKOA Nats, as well as at the 20th.

(1972–1974), I credit him for featuring lowriders two or three times, but that's as close as any other magazine, besides *Street Rodder*, came to featuring any kind of custom cars during the entire decade of the 1970s.

By the July 1978 issue of *Street Rodder*, we featured Richard Zocchi's gorgeous *Cool 50* Merc on the cover, with the main blurb: "The New Trend—Street Customs." Inside, beside's Zocchi's,

we featured another chopped '51 Merc, a '58 Impala mild custom, and a chopped '56 Olds four-door with big fins. A six-page article titled "Street Customs," illustrated by Steve Stanford, showed and discussed examples of the types of 1950s-style mild customs rodders could be building: '57 Plymouth and '54 Chevy hardtops, '56 Olds, '57 Ford, '60 Pontiac, '58 and '60 Impalas, and even a pinch-fender F-100. This was the first magazine illustration or design Stanford had ever done.

Even though no magazines were pushing it after that, the revival of 1950s-style customs continued to build. Jerry Titus of Wichita, Kansas, who worked for Darryl Starbird as a "sand boy" for a time, courted his wife, De Vona,

One of the few early customs to show at Wichita was Conrad Winkler's scalloped '51 Olds convertible that was on little magazine covers in 1959. It was in its original, unrestored form in 1981—but we haven't seen it since.

One of the first to revive the early custom style was well-known car builder Sam Foose, who built this maroon, flathead-powered, chop-top '47 Ford in the latter 1970s and drove the wheels off of it.

Another early-look custom '47 Ford was this maroon convertible with a Carson-style top and Caddy grille from somewhere in NorCal. It used to attend late 1970s and early 1980s rod events. Haven't seen it for at least a decade.

in a chopped '50 Merc. Citing the 1977 chopped Merc issue of *Street Rodder* as at least partial inspiration, he decided to stage an event just for '49–'51 Mercurys. He was going to call it a "Reunion." But in discussing his plans with Starbird, by then a seasoned show producer, Jerry explicitly remembers Starbird's words: "There aren't 10 Mercurys in America." Jerry's solution was to add '32 Fords to the mix—the classic hot rod and the classic custom—and call it the Merc-Deuce Reunion. He held the first one in the parking lot of the Kansas City Dragway. He said 383 Mercs and Deuces showed for the three-day event, including about 25 chopped Mercs. But he lost his shorts.

It took Jerry a few months to recover from this event, both financially and emotionally. But he had a pretty substantial mailing list that he had compiled to promote the reunion, and by early 1980 he typed up a letter asking if there was any interest in a custom car association, and sent it out. He got enough positive response that he put an ad in the Antique/Classic Car classifieds of the *Wichita Eagle & Beacon* newspaper, asking anyone interested in forming/joining such an association to meet at the Park Villa recreation building on October 1, 1980. Twelve people showed, including Hub Harness of the Fundamentals club. All joined, and they pulled numbers from a hat to see what their charter numbers would be.

Jerry said he had a bit of a problem calling it a custom car association, because that would exclude pickups. He said he thought about it for a while, and "Being a '50s cat," came up with the term "kemp" (a beatnik term for your car, your wheels, your "short"). And of course Kustom had to be spelled with a K, in best Barris fashion. Thus the Kustom Kemps of America (KKOA) was born. The initial rules were that customized vehicles from 1935 through 1964 would be allowed as members.

The first big KKOA event, the Leadsled Spectacular, was staged in a grassy, hilly park adjacent to the Kansas Coliseum in Wichita on August 6–9, 1981. I wrote a six-page freelance article on it that appeared in the December 1981 issue of *Hot Rod* magazine. The short copy said, "A revived interest in early-style customs has been swelling for the past few years," and suggested that customs, "built for comfort, not for speed," might be better suited to those gas-shortage times than hot rods. Approximately 400 customs, "some old, some new" attended from all over the country. What is very important to note is that not only did the custom car revival finally have a national organization, and a "national" event, but it received major coverage in a magazine with nearly 1,000,000 readers, rather than one with a little over 100,000.

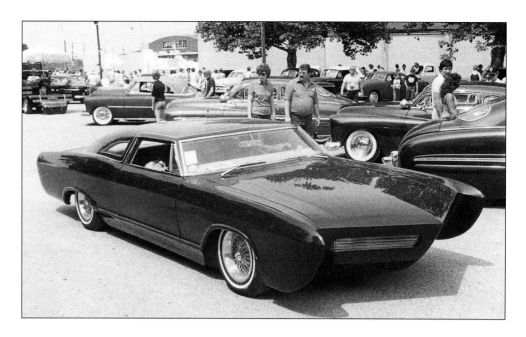

One very interesting thing to note about that initial event is that, with only a few exceptions, all of the entrants were recently built cars, done almost exclusively in the 1950s style. One notable exception was Bob Drake's restoration of Jack Stewart's '41 Ford. Starbird had his bubble top *Predicta* T-bird on

Lee Pratt never stopped building custom cars. He did this wild rendition of a '65 Buick LeSabre from a Harry Bradley design in candy wild cherry in the mid-1970s. He undoubtedly had the only chopped full custom on hydraulics cruising Des Moines, Iowa, at that time.

The problem with Pratt's '65 Buick was that it couldn't attend pre-1949-only events, so he built this purple '41 Buick fastback, also riding on full hydraulics, and had it at the first KKOA meet.

There were a lot of custom '36 Ford convertibles and three-windows—some with LaSalle grilles—in the Pacific Northwest. Eric Perkins of Montesano, Washington, found this black beauty, with padded top, ripple bumpers, solid hood, and abbreviated running boards, just like this, and is keeping it this way.

You'd never know Larry Purcell's black lacquer '41 Ford from Colorado Springs has a modern Ford small block under the hood. Built in pure 1940s style, it was at Wichita in 1981.

The custom car revival was definitely not a Southern California thing. One of the first in Southern California was Mel Becker's tasteful candy red flathead-powered '50 Ford sedan that showed up in the late 1970s.

hand. And there was one '40 Merc done in the Matranga style.

I continued to cover the Spectacular as a *Hot Rod* staffer for the next several years, until I became editor of the revived *Rod & Custom*, where I continued coverage, as well as featuring customs along with the rods, as in the old days.

In the Winter of 1991, McMullen-Yee Publishing revived its *Custom Rodder* title, with Jerry Weesner as editor, and relegated coverage of all post–1948 vehicles to it, customs and otherwise. There hadn't been a whole lot of custom coverage in *Street Rodder* in the 1980s, but this pretty much squelched it.

This brings up a couple of things to think about before we close this chapter. First, in the June 1986 issue of *Hot Rod* magazine, I did an eight-page article on custom cars, subtitled "Is It Time to Rethink the Custom?" That article said: "I'm afraid this latter-day Leadsled/Kustom Kemp movement may be Kandy-painting itself into a corner—festooned with fuzzy dice, dummy spots, lakes pipes, fender skirts, flipper hubcaps, and flame-throwing exhaust pipes. Such customs

can be cool, for sure; but there are plenty of other things custom cars can—and should—be."

In subsequent years we did start to see some excellent examples of high-tech or new-wave customs, incorporating components seen on contemporary street rods, such as billet wheels, blackwalls, no skirts or sidepipes, more modern upholstery materials, and more street rod–like engine detailing. Some dyed-in-the-wool customizers can't stand this look, but I think it should be part of the mix. However, it's still being done primarily on 1950s-1960s body styles. In the day, customs were new or near-new cars. Why is virtually no one customizing new cars today? Think of a recent T-Bird or Lincoln lowered, dechromed, candy-colored, with maybe some headlight, taillight, or bumper changes. Even the KKOA has dropped its 1964 cut-off year to include newer cars. A few people have tried customizing late models, but they either start with the wrong, boxy models, they chop the top way too much, or they go off on other tangents that don't complement the car's lines. I'm talking simple mild customizing: shave it, smooth it, drop it, add some custom wheels, and coat it with a striking organic paint job.

The second consideration is that there are plenty of 1950s and 1960s cars available today at

very affordable prices. A lot of people seem to think that any modified 1950s or early 1960s car is a custom. Not so. Just like '40 Fords, you can build them as rods or as customs. When we relaunched *Rod & Custom* magazine, I really pushed building 1950s cars as rods. A lot of people never got it. Some people totally disagree, but I say that a car that sits on a rake, has big 'n' little blackwall tires, mag wheels, and no skirts, sidepipes, or spot lights, is not a custom. It might be nosed and decked. It might have tuck-and-roll upholstery. But it's a rod, not a custom. In the 1960s we didn't call them hot rods, they were just "cars." But they had a tach on the dash, four on the floor, some belled "cheater" pipes dangling under the rear axle, maybe even some cheater slicks.

This chopped, shaved, and frenched '46 Chevy was first built as a street rod. When Jim Walker of Dayton, Ohio, added it to his excellent early custom collection in the mid-1980s, he lowered it in the back, added skirts, spots, and whitewalls, then painted it black to make it a 1940s-style custom.

Dick Dean has been popping out customs since he was a kid in Detroit. He did this very purple '40 Merc sort of Matranga-style for a customer in Oregon in the 1980s when his shop was in Fullerton, California.

Jim Wilkins found this sectioned '51 Ford Vicky rusting in a backyard, half-finished, in 1980. After lots of rebuilding, he had it on the new custom scene by 1983.

Don "The Egyptian" Boeke from nearby Dayton, Ohio, had this tasty candy tangerine '57 Ford mild custom at Springfield in 1983.

Same as when they were new, the longer, lower cars of the late 1950s need less customizing. Larry Simonutti's low '60 Pontiac hardtop has frenched lights, custom grille bars, louvers in the rockers, and appropriate Astro Supreme wheels.

Guitarist Jimmie Vaughan is a real 1960s custom enthusiast, with three in his garage right now. He had this mild '51 Fleetline done in purple primer in 1988, but by 1990 he had Gary Howard restyle it and paint it like this.

Young Tony Jobson of Mattydale, New York, bought a restored '50 Chevy Fleetline at the Hershey swap meet in 1985 and turned it into this slick purple pearl custom with ghost flames by 1993.

A case in point is the '53 Chevy project car I built at *Rod & Custom*. As featured in its final form in the November 1993 issue, it was nosed and decked, had a custom-peaked hood and recessed rear license, shaved bumpers, custom grille and taillights, and a lush pearl paint job. But it also had polished American five-spokes with big 'n' little blackwalls, it sat on a pronounced rake, it had Mooneyes gauges, an aluminum steering wheel, and a floorshift. It had door handles and all its stock side chrome, and a billetized dual-quad small block under the hood. Some might not call this car a rod, but it just as certainly isn't a custom.

Right

As I said, the custom car revival was not a California deal. However, since the early 1980s, the West Coast Kustoms gathering in Paso Robles, on Highway 101 halfway between Los Angeles and San Francisco, has become the preeminent California custom gathering, with cars crowding the city park by day and cruising the A&W drive-in (seen here) at night.

Being the first big car show of the year in California, the Oakland Roadster Show had been the coming-out event for new customs by the likes of Richard Zocchi, John D'Agostino, and others for a couple of decades. This arena scene from 1994 shows Zocchi's pearl yellow chopped '51 Olds next to D'Agostino's *Stardust* '39 Merc, with Frank Livingston's pearl blue chopped Merc, built mostly by Paul Bragg, in the foreground.

CHAPTER
NINE

Since it was finished first (in the early 1980s), we'll show Jack Walker's well-known Hirohata Merc clone from Belton, Missouri, first. Built as exact to the original, with Cadillac engine, as they could determine from existing magazine articles, it was constructed by Doug Thompson. Jack has shown and driven it so much over the years he has had to restore it at least once.

CLONES AND RESTORATIONS

IT'S SURPRISING TO NOTE

how few clones and restorations of famous early customs there were at the beginning of the custom car revival. On the other hand, what is many times more amazing is how many famous customs from the 1940s, 1950s, and 1960s have been found, and are actually available for restoration.

Some of the now-restored famous (or not famous) early customs were discovered completely by accident. Such is the case of Joe Eddy's Ayala-built Wally Welch '50 Merc. After the chopped Merc issue of *Street Rodder* came out, the son of a neighbor across the street, who was into hot rods, kept telling Eddy that he knew where one of these cars was, in someone's backyard. Eddy kept thinking, "Yeah, some old Hudson, or something." Then, when the next Merc issue hit, with Zocchi's *Cool '50* on the cover, the kid came back over with the magazine, saying, "The car I've been telling you about looks just like this one." That got Eddy's attention. The kid led Eddy to the Lincoln Heights area of Los Angeles and, sure enough, under an avocado tree out behind the garage behind a house, sat an early chopped '50 Merc. It was covered with corrugated metal sheeting, and someone had painted it with white house paint for protection, though Eddy could see some purple wearing back through along the bottom. The owner said it had last run in 1957 (it had a Y-block Ford engine in it), and he wanted $3,500 for it. Eddy said, "No, it's going to take a lot of work to rebuild it." So the guy came down significantly on the price, and Eddy hauled it away. He even got it running the next week, and drove it to an event, before tearing it down for a full rebuild. He said the car was quite complete, with all the windows, handles, trim pieces, and so on. In fact, Eddy is the third owner of the car.

Eddy had no idea of the car's identity at first, but he thought he remembered it from some little magazines. He started searching, and found it on the cover of the April 1952 *Hop Up*, painted lime green with four De Soto teeth in the grille. Barris later painted it purple and added two more teeth. At the time Eddy got the car, exact restoration of a historied early custom didn't seem so important. He restored

Long-time rodder Joe Eddy of Temple City, California, stumbled upon the Ayala-built Wally Welch Merc sitting in someone's backyard under an avocado tree about 15 years ago. He didn't even know the car's history until after he started rebuilding it.

Here's a young Spence Murray, *Rod & Custom*'s first editor, with the *Dream Truck* when it was first finished in its white and purple version, with fins.

Far right
Here's Spence with the *Dream Truck* as restored by Carl Green for Bruce Glasscock at the first KKOA Nats in 1981.

the exterior of the car faithfully, but added a modern driveline, gray cloth interior, and amenities like power steering, air conditioning, and stereo sound. He drives it frequently.

Just to put the up-and-down interest in customs in perspective, here's another story that might be related to Eddy's find. I was talking to Jerry Weesner about the drawings he did for that very first chopped Merc issue of *Street Rodder* (November 1974). He said I had assigned him to draw the "how to chop a Merc" illustrations, but that he had already drawn the four famous Mercs, so he obviously had an interest in early customs (unlike most rodders at the time). However, he was more interested in '40 Fords,

being a member of Forties Limited. Not long before that issue, he answered an ad to go see, and ultimately buy, a '40 sedan somewhere in the Los Angeles area. The owner asked Jerry if he had any interest in a Barris chopped Merc, because he had one out behind the garage that he wanted to sell. Jerry asked if it ran. The guy said no. So Jerry said he wasn't interested. He has no idea what car it was, because he didn't even walk around the garage to look at it! He was much more interested in the '40 Ford. But this might be the same Merc that Joe Eddy got.

Other famous early customs have been the subjects of long and arduous searches. One such is the *Rod & Custom Dream Truck*. Most anyone reading this book knows it was wrecked in a towing accident 90 miles west of Wichita on the way to a show in Des Moines, Iowa, in 1958. Both the lead '58 Chevy pickup, driven by owner and *R&C* Editor Spence Murray, and the flat-towed *Dream Truck* flipped into a corn field. The *Dream Truck* was severely damaged. Spence had the remains shipped back to California, where Barris gave him an estimate of $3,500 (those are 1958 dollars), unpainted, to fix it. So Spence sold what he could—engine, driveline, wheels, gauges—and sold the remains to somebody in Pasadena for

$150. He said it changed hands several more times at that same price, then disappeared. After Spence returned as *R&C* editor in 1967, he and Dave Puhl tried to track the truck down once again, unsuccessfully. A year later, writer Michael

And here's Spence with the *Dream Truck* as re-restored by Kurt McCormick recently.

Mickey Ellis' '39 Merc, which is actually the ex-Don Telen car, parks next to Larry Purcell's black '41 at KKOA Number 1 in 1981. The car now belongs to Lynn "C.W. Moss" Williams, in the same condition.

By far the best Matranga clone so far is this one created by Bill Hines for Duncan Emmons of Rancho Mirage, California. Besides the rich maroon paint, it has accurate Eddie Martinez upholstery and a Joe Reath flathead.

Between the first and second KKOA Nats, "Top Chop Charlie" Brewer of Hamilton, Ohio, built this exact replica of the *Moonglow* '54 Chevy. I'm not sure if this photo was taken before or after it was stolen for a year. When we featured it in the first issue of *The Rodder's Journal* in 1994, it was owned by Tony Feil of Raritan, New Jersey.

The paint was done in a last-minute rush to make a museum show in Oakland by Junior at his shop, where some "helpers" dropped by. That's George Barris with a crest, Junior with spray gun, Frank Sonzogni with hammer and file, Jim with the pink slip, and Bill Larzalere with buffer. The color was matched in lacquer to the original paint on the car by PPG headquarters in Detroit.

Lamm sent in some photos of a crudely hammered-out *Dream Truck* located somewhere in Stockton, California, in someone's yard.

Using these photos and a general description of where the neighborhood was, Bruce Glascock said he literally started going door-to-door trying to locate it—and he did! But the owner wouldn't sell. Bruce said he called every three months for eight years before the owner, who had pounded the truck out with a sledge hammer but obviously couldn't take the restoration further, finally relented. When it crashed, Bruce said the truck had "pirouetted on its right front fender, then slammed on its left side, bending the driver's door backward." He also said that, for as much as it had been through and how long it sat, it was actually pretty complete and still wore its last gold and purple Barris paint job. He took the truck home to Westminster, California, where Spence Murray helped arrange for metalman Carl Green and a helper to come out from Bartlesville,

Oklahoma, to repair the body, using some pieces from a donor pickup.

Once finished in primer, it went back to Oklahoma for new paint in the white/purple scallops scheme, and then on the Starbird show circuit for a year. Glascock got it back in time to take it to the first KKOA Spectacular in Wichita,

And now for the real thing. Jim McNiel has owned the original Hirohata Merc since he was 16. He drove it on the street for several years, then stored it in his garage until we announced the beginning of its restoration in the August 1989 issue of *R&C*. It took Jim until 1998 to finish it.

137

and then drove it many thousands of miles before selling it to Kurt McCormick in 1985. McCormick did a full restoration of the chassis, driveline, and interior, retaining the pearl white that was on the body, but redoing the purple scallops. The fact that this custom truck is still with us after all that is pretty amazing.

The fact that the Nick Matranga Merc coupe and the *Moonglow* '54 Chevy aren't with us has, I think, been one of the reasons that these are the two most-cloned customs of all, especially the Matranga Merc. I've already related how Duane Steck's brother watched the *Moonglow* crushed. The Matranga Merc was sold by Nick's mother while he was overseas in Korea, sometime around 1950–1951. The common story, that I have heard from several people, is that the new owner was street racing it, possibly on a stormy night, lost

There are plenty of white and powder blue copies of the *Moonglow*, so custom painter Richard Glymph of Maryland painted his in these richer colors in the early 1980s.

Given the description of its condition (in the text), the restoration of the Barris-built Rev. Ernst Chevy must have been a Herculean task. It took owner Burns Berryman and metalman Jack Florence 10 years to rebuild it.

Keith Ashley's clone of the second version of the Ernst Chevy, begun by John Kouw in Holland, Michigan, and finished by Randy Church Restorations in St. Charles, Michigan, is just stunning—and very likely finished better than the Barris version ever was.

Seeing these two cars side-by-side is a treat, but it also demonstrates the rear-end differences between the two versions, as well as a few subtle changes suggested by Harry Bradley on the clone, such as lowering the spare tire.

Speaking of Harry Bradley, his *La Jolla* '51 Chevy, inspired by the Ernst car, designed by Harry on notebook paper, and built by New York customizer Herb Gary in 1955, has recently been acquired and restored (again, with some "improvements" suggested—and designed—by Bradley) by Jack Walker. In this case the restoration was relatively easy, as Bradley kept the car in good condition since new.

control, and wrapped it around a power pole. In fact, in an article for *Street Rodder* magazine on the car, for which he interviewed Matranga, Greg Sharp said: "Sometime in early 1952, the new owner was street racing . . . on a rainy night in San Pedro. He lost control crossing slippery railroad tracks and wrapped the custom around a

telephone pole. The driver walked away, but the Merc wasn't as lucky. The dash was buckled, and the remainder was declared a total loss." We presume the car is gone. It certainly has never been seen since.

However, the stories never fail to amaze me. One of the first "near clones" of the Matranga car was owned by Utah hot rod illustrator Mickey Ellis. I had recalled that he had built it from an early custom that had been wrecked, so I called to ask him the story. Yes, he said, this car turned out to be the same one that was featured in the March 1957 *Hot Rod* when it belonged to Don Telen of Oregon. I vividly remember this car because by 1957 it was already an anachronism. There just weren't any customs like this still around. Hot rodder/bookseller Neal East said he knew Telen when they were both attending

Jack Walker's latest clone is of Lyle Lake's *Blue Danube* '51 Buick. Kenny Baker of Elmer, Missouri, chopped the top and Dick Huckans of Sperry, Oklahoma, finished the bodywork and paint. We're glad he didn't go with the drawer-knob grille version. With this car, the Hirohata clone, and the Polynesian clone in his stable, Jack has earned the reputation of "King of the Clones."

Brigham Young University, and maybe that's how the car got to Salt Lake City. But Ellis said that his car, along with a full custom '51 Chevy, sat in the basement of a parking garage in Salt Lake, abandoned, for nearly 10 years. Plenty of area rodders knew about them, but nobody had any interest. The Merc was severely crunched from a head-on collision, and the rear end had been hit several times. There are some twists here involving various owners of the parking structure, a sudden escalation of the "value" of the car, and Lynn "C.W. Moss" Williams (who first purchased it). Ellis finally acquired the wreck in 1975, and he and fellow Stags club member Brent Bodily rebuilt it. They started by cutting the whole front end off at the windshield (the front fenders had been welded to the body) and installing a new front end. Ellis said if he had known it was

the Telen car, he might have rebuilt it as such. Instead, he painted it a deep maroon, like the Matranga Merc, with bubble skirts. The only major difference is that it doesn't have the curved side window frames. Ellis had this car at the first KKOA Leadsled Spectacular. After many years, he sold it back to Lynn Williams, and it is now in Doug Hall's growing early custom collection.

One of the better Matranga Merc clones is John D'Agostino's *Stardust*. Built in 1988, it has

Continued on page 147

The undisputed king of Barris restorations is Kurt McCormick of Webster Groves, Missouri. This photo was taken when he still had the Jim Seaton '55 Chevy, the Zaro Merc was unrestored, and he didn't yet have the Alcorn Merc. The *Dr.'s Roadster* in the foreground was built at Valley Custom. The '41 Carson-top Buick on the right was built by Barris in 1955 for Herb Ogden. Restored by Barry Mazza, it was acquired in this form by Kurt recently.

When you see the "before" photos of this one, you'll be amazed it could look like this today. Jim Walker of Dayton, Ohio, had metalman Dave Oakes graft the original Sam Barris Buick body onto a low-mile original '50 Buick chassis and floorpan. Kurt has had this car many years.

WHERE DID THE
ORIGINAL CUSTOMS GO?

This may seem repetitious, but given the all-but-complete death of traditional custom cars for nearly 20 years, it is truly astounding that so many are still around, in one form or another. Hot rods are different. They're smaller; they don't take up so much storage space. They're easy to take apart and put back together. They don't deteriorate as badly as customs. But customs, in the first place, are more stylized than rods, so they go out of style more quickly, and they are harder to update. They're big and bulky. And they crack and peel.

Some of the restorations, such as the Sam Barris Buick, the Cushenbery-built *El Matador* '40 Ford, the *R&C Dream Truck*, and the Barris-built Rev. Ernst Chevy have been Herculean rebuilds of cars that were crashed, smashed, left to rot on the ground, or even burned (or all of the above).

But others, such as the Wally Welch Merc, were somewhat protected while stored outside in a mild climate. Recently I saw the Valley Custom Ron Dunn sectioned '50 Ford, still in its '58 or so bronze paint, upholstery, and "towel rack" taillights, sitting in someone's driveway just a couple miles from where the car was built. The paint had flaked in a couple of spots, with mild surface rust forming. The owner (I think one of Dunn's relatives) has had the car for decades; I hope he's put it back in the garage.

While it's kind of hard to store a custom in your home garage (though Jim McNiel did it—you wouldn't believe what all he has in there), I think most have been stashed away in corners of bigger shops—especially body, paint, or custom shops. I guess if you're into this type of work, you have an appreciation for good (or extensive) custom work in the first place, and you can't stand to see it thrown away. But if you're running a

professional shop, your personal projects have to take secondary importance. After it sat behind Bill Hines' shop for years (along with other aging customs) with some body damage, the Buddy Alcorn Merc was stored (again outside, though wrapped up) for another couple decades by custom painter Ron Jones, before Kurt McCormick finally acquired it and restored it. Last I heard, the original Polynesian sectioned Olds was sitting in a custom shop called The Red Lacquer Room somewhere in Ohio (or Indiana?), with some sort of fins added to the rear fenders. Jim Skonzakis (now known as Jim Street) still has both the *Kookie* T and the *Golden Sahara* in storage, and not too long ago asked someone to give him an estimate on restoring the latter. The person declined, not so much because of the car's condition, but because of all the electronics involved and some questionable under-the-skin original construction. And you see some photos here of the *Trendero* '57 Ranchero, in amazingly complete condition, slowly decomposing in the back of the big Chicago Trend Kustom shop where it was originally built.

Of course, many of the famous customs are long gone. I can't remember all the exact details, but Joe Bailon told me that his *Miss Elegance* Chevy first sat on the corner of a used car lot to attract customers' attention. Sometime later it was acquired by someone who parked it in the driveway next to his house where his kids played on it, sliding from the roof of the house onto the roof of the car. Next, the car went to someone who put a Chrysler Hemi in it, jacked up the front end, and cut out the rear fenders so wide tires could stick out. With the hood off, he street raced it until the wife said it had to go. Then the car disappeared.

But years later, some friends of Bailon's were driving by a lady's house, and there was the chrome dash from *Miss Elegance*, with all the gauges, sitting in the front yard, either in a yard sale or in a pile of trash she was throwing out. The ends of the dash had been cut off to put it in some smaller car. The lady had no information as to where it came from. But they acquired it and gave it back to Bailon, who is now building a clone of the car.

In Chapter 1 you saw the Ray Vega '38 convertible sedan, built by Valley Custom. Yes, this is the same car, seen at the Los Angeles Roadsters show about 20 years ago. Rolls-Royce restorer Tony Handler said he rescued it from an impound lot in 1963, where it sat with a crunched left front fender, awaiting further crushing. He cut out the fenders and added slicks during the many years he's had it, but it's now being refinished in black with a black top and flathead power.

This '39 convertible sedan was on the Los Angeles rod scene 20-some years ago, first in primer with an old top, then in black paint with a new white top, then—gone again.

Here's a killer for you. Any of you of age will remember the yellow *Trendero* '57 Ford Ranchero, built by John Malik and Dave Puhl at Trend Custom shop on the outskirts of Chicago in 1961. About 1991, Miles Masa took me to an old, junky body shop, and in the back, under plastic wraps, this is what we found—dirty, decaying, but complete to the booze bottles in the bed. The place? Trend Body Shop. Probably still there.

I took this picture of the Bailon *Candy Bird* at the Los Angeles Roadsters show/swap when it was at the Great Western Exhibit Center in the 1970s. Next I got a letter at *R&C*, with photos, from a guy who had it in Mississippi (1991). Now it's back in California, slated to be restored by Bailon himself.

On that same trip to Chicago in 1991, these are just a couple of other gems Miles led me to, just sitting in people's garages. And there are plenty more just like them, famous or not, that I have shown in the pages of *Street Rodder* and *Rod & Custom* over the years. Some get rebuilt, others just rust.

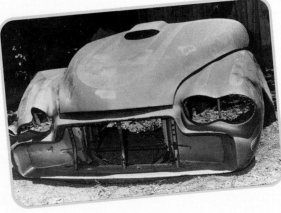

These photos, taken by Mike Lamm on a street in Stockton, California, in the late 1970s, were what finally led Bruce Glasscock to the remains of the *Dream Truck*. It looks better than it is—you can't see the sledge-hammer and slide-puller "repair work." It's incredible that this thing survived and lives today.

Discovered by Bob McCormick near Taunton, Massachusetts, this is how the Barris Buick sat. Chris Carrier pulled it out of the weeds, then Jim Walker bought it and had it restored. No small task.

This is how the Alcorn Merc looked when it arrived at McCormick's after 40 years of outdoor storage. It actually looks much better than it was.

Looks can also be very deceiving. The first photo shows the Zaro Merc as McCormick received it from Duluth, complete and driveable. The second shows everything Kurt threw away after finding most of the car was galvanized sheetmetal pop-riveted together with buckets of Bondo on top. The frame fell apart when he cut the sheet metal away. The only parts he saved were the roof, chrome dash with laminated knobs, the shift knob, and pink slip.

Kurt's latest find is in better condition and will be his next project. This chopped '41 Cad convertible with fadeaways was built by Harry Westergard for Al Laver.

Now get this. Guy Boucher of Lewiston, Maine, had just finished a near clone of the Hirohata Merc and decided to build a '32 roadster. He called Brookville Roadster to buy a body and got to talking with the Gollahons (owners) about Barris customs. "Oh, we have one of those," they said. Turned out 92-year old Grandma Gollahon bought *El Capitola* 40-some years ago for a grandson who likes karate more than cars. She's kept it perfect all this time: paint, upholstery, chrome. Somebody painted the red part gold for some reason, so Guy (who obviously got the car) will repaint that and freshen the 30,000-mile driveline. They're out there. Go get them.

You saw the Zaro and Andril Mercs together in Chapter 1. This is the Zaro car, which Kurt located and had Dave Conrad rebuild in '54 Buick Titian red paint to a level far superior to the original. Kurt says this car had five different grille treatments over the years, including a Vega!

Continued from page 141

the curved window frames, red Lucite taillights in the rear bumper guards, and a dressed flathead engine, but it differs in areas such as an extended and peaked hood, molded-off running boards, hidden hinges, and more modern upholstery.

Undoubtedly the most accurate Matranga clone is Duncan Emmons', built recently by Bill Hines, with an Eddie Martinez maroon and white tuck-and-roll interior and a mild, two-carb flathead built by Joe Reath. Even the license plates match Matranga's. There are several others, possibly a dozen or more, in varying degrees of likeness to the original.

The other much-cloned custom is the *Moonglow* '54 Chevy. Admittedly, this is an easier car to build, the primary modification being the top chop. But it is still a highly engaging custom—one of the classics. It was included as one of the Top 20 All-Time Rods and Customs in the August 1990 issue of *R&C*. One of the first like-

nesses was Richard Glymph's, though he simply frenched the stock taillights, and (probably because he's a custom painter) changed the colors to a rich maroon body with a silver top.

Probably the most exact re-creation of the car is Tony Feil's from Raritan, New Jersey, originally built by "Top Chop Charlie" Brewer of Hamilton, Ohio, in the early 1980s. There are a couple of minor inconsistencies, such as the fully peaked hood and the pleated inserts in the interior, but otherwise it's exact, also down to the

This '54 Eldorado, called the *Parisienne*, was customized new for supermarket executive Milton Melton of Los Angeles. Bohman and Schwartz of Pasadena made the lift-off landau top with brass castings and trim, as well as an aluminum deck lid. Barris did the rest of the custom work, including the inset Continental kit. Kurt got the car in 1978, less top and hood, but didn't have Dave Conrad restore it until 1993–1994.

Kurt's latest Barris save—and it was a big job—is the Buddy Alcorn Merc. Again beautifully restored by Dave Conrad, this car was initially chopped in 1952 by the Ayalas, then finished for Alcorn by the Barrises in 1955. Sometime after 1957, it got hit on the driver side, and sat that way on Harold Mabe's car lot "for a few years," according to Kurt (and where Jim and Sue McNiel considered buying it for Sue to drive—but didn't). Kurt debuted it at the 20th anniversary KKOA Spectacular in 2000.

license plates. One of the most amazing stories about this car is that it was stolen from Brewer's yard, was gone for a full year, and was then spotted parked on a rural road outside of town. He simply went out and drove it home. It had one scratch on it.

Besides Charlie's, there were two other *Moonglow* clones at the second KKOA Spectacular in Des Moines, two done in white and blue. I have seen about eight, total. One of the nicest was built by Bill Layman of Pennsylvania. Layman's was identical in body modifications, and he painted his a bright blue metallic all over—

but so did Steck in one of the original car's later iterations. And speaking of restorations, Layman also found and fully restored the Fred Rowe '51 Merc convertible built by Barris, which co-starred in *Running Wild* with the Hirohata Merc.

Speaking of which, the latter is probably the most celebrated example of both a clone and a restoration in the custom car universe. Most of us into early customs had heard—and of course believed—the rumor that the original car existed, but that it was owned by some weirdo who was hoarding it in his garage, and wouldn't let anybody see it, let alone divulge his, or its, whereabouts. In fact, I knew a couple of people who had seen the car, knew where it was, but wouldn't tell me—for years. In one instance, the owner had literally been offered a grocery bag full of cash for the car, and he turned it down.

Since we're discussing near-clones here, as well as exact ones, I should back up a bit and mention that Steve Gonzales' bronze Merc, seen on the cover of that 1977 chopped Merc issue of *Street Rodder*, is patterned very closely on the Hirohata car other than color, side chrome, curved side window moldings, and grille. Gonzales still has this car.

Jack Walker, of Belton, Missouri, on the other hand, wanted the Hirohata Merc, just the way he saw

One of the first custom clones I saw was this '46 Ford from Michigan called *Arctic Gold*, which attended rod nats in the mid-1970s. The original, called *Arctic Sand*, was built by Clarkaiser in Detroit for Ken Peterson of Lake Orion, Michigan, and appeared on the July 1957 *R&C* cover. I haven't seen the clone in 20-some years.

You saw Jack Stewart's chopped and sectioned Ford coupe in the opening chapter. Sometime after Jim Skonzakis bought it and took it to Ohio, it got hit by a train. Bob Drake of Indiana got the car and miraculously restored it in the 1970s, as seen here at the first KKOA meet.

Two brothers in the San Francisco East Bay built near-identical custom '40 Chevy convertibles in the early 1950s. Ron Brooks of Castro Valley found this one with a '53 Chevy grille in the mid-1970s, restored it beautifully in rich maroon, and has been driving it ever since.

It's surprising how some of these cars come and go. This Carson-top convertible sedan with the Chevy grille and quad lights showed up at rod meets in SoCal in the mid-to-latter 1970s, first in primer, then in paint—then it vanished.

it in early 1950s car mags. So, knowing he couldn't buy the original, he built his own with the help of ace metalman Doug Thompson, in 1985. Working strictly from magazine photos (from Kurt McCormick's collection), they built as exact a replica as possible. There were a few things they couldn't have known, such as the two different colors of green in the interior, because all they had were black and white photos to go by (though Jack thinks this might have been a later change). Other items, such as the twin aerials in the back fenders, and the single four-barrel on the Cad engine, are more accurate than the real car today. Thompson even hammered the correct numbers and letters into an early California license plate to match Hirohata's in 1952. As custom cars go, I would say this one is king of the clones. Besides his restored Ray Fahrner *Eclipse* and the recently restored Harry Bradley *La Jolla*, Walker has also cloned the Lyle Lake *Blue Danube* Barris '52 Buick.

However, the real Hirohata Merc is unquestionably king of the customs. Why? Let me quote from an article I wrote in *The Rodder's Journal* Number 5, when current owner Jim McNiel fired up and drove the car for the first time in 30 years: "Why was the Hirohata Merc the star of that era? What made it so famous? This car took the smooth, streamlined, 'organic' postwar custom style perfected by the Barrises and the Ayalas to the next level. I have quoted Harry Bradley before as saying that the Hirohata Merc was the best of the overcustomized Mercs. It was also the first. It was the first chopped '51 Merc, arguably the first car design to hint at the coming 'fin' age, and definitely sleeker than the round-tailed '49–'50s. The pale, pastel ice green paint was so different from Barris' typical rich, lush metallic lacquers that the color added further impact. And even small details like the green and white laminated plastic

The stories of some of these existing customs are amazing. Lore Sharp of Bremerton, Washington, decided to section his '56 Buick after it was wrecked in 1958. Bodyman Gil Clifford did the job and painted it candy red. In this form, with chrome wheels and baby moons, it was one of *Car Craft's* 10 Best Customs, February 1962. Then, during the bubble top craze (1965), Sharp took the car to Cushenbery's, who cut the top off. But it never got further, and ended up in Clifford's shop (along with the severed top) for about 25 years. Then Paul Harper of Roslyn, Washington, got it, welded the top back on, and rebuilt it with wire wheels, bucket seats, and metallic maroon paint as seen in 1990. Recently new owners acquired it and decided they wanted to "personalize" it some more with new paint and other changes. Oh well.

While the original is supposedly rusting away, John Ballard of Anderson, Indiana, decided to build his own clone of the famous Valley Custom *Polynesian* sectioned '50 Olds. With the help of friend Gary Rafe, he built and painted it himself— no small job—keeping everything true to original, other than a '76 Seville front clip and modified Olds 455 engine. A few years back he drove it to Paso Robles, where he received Neil Emory's blessing. Now Jack Walker owns it.

While Roth put most of his cars in Jim Brucker's "Cars of the Stars" museum, and they went from there to Harrah's (where the *Outlaw* and *Beatnik Bandit* got restored, and the rest got auctioned), the trails of others are circuitous. This is the VW-powered *Wishbone*, which Roth actually cut in half and threw away, but which Roth's helper, Dirty Doug, rescued and welded back together sometime in the 1970s. In the 1990s one of Roth's sons somehow acquired it, rebuilt it in this form (different paint, wheels, tires), then— poof!—it was gone again.

teardrop dash knobs, which Hirohata made himself, started a fad that persists today. It was an amazingly impressive vehicle in 1952, and it immediately began winning car show trophies (supposedly 184 overall) and covers and feature pages in magazines. But what helped elevate this car to legendary status were feats such as Bob's

cross-country trip to the Indianapolis car show chronicled in the October 1953 issue of *Rod & Custom*, the big first-place trophy it won there, and its costarring role in the 1955 teen flick *Running Wild* with Keenan Wynn and Mamie Van Doren."

I've already mentioned that 16-year-old Jim McNiel bought the well-used custom off a lot for $500 in 1959 or 1960. He dated his wife, Sue, in it, and even used it to drop her off at work after they were married. The fact that Sue has as much interest in the car, and pitched in with its restoration (as did their son, Scott), probably had something to do with its being saved in the family garage all these years.

When I finally got Jim McNiel's name and phone number (I think it was Greg Sharp who relented and gave it to me), I called and asked if we could make the car's restoration a project for

Rod & Custom magazine. McNiel said no. I explained that he could do all the work himself, at his house, but that we could get him most of the parts and materials he needed at no cost. That got McNiel's attention. We announced the car's "uncovering" in the August 1989 issue.

McNiel is no wierdo. He's a multitalented craftsman who can do just about anything on a car. Several companies or people did contribute to the project, including Mr. Merc, Egge Machine, Fat Man Fabrications, Verne's Plating, and PPG paints. But the project moved very slowly as McNiel completed each operation himself: building and installing the engine, welding the exhaust system, repairing and reinforcing the frame, aligning the front end, and so on. After more than five years, I hinted strongly to McNiel that my days at *R&C* were numbered, but that didn't hurry him. It was a promised appearance at the Hot Rods and

Customs show at the Oakland Museum in September 1996 that finally set a deadline, and Hershel "Junior" Conway volunteered at the 11th hour to paint the car with lacquers matched to the original colors by PPG headquarters. Several of us pitched in to help with the frenzied—but perfect—paint job. Then McNiel traded a 3.8 Jag sedan he had in his backyard to Eddie Martinez to restitch the interior to match the remains of the original Carson/Gaylord upholstery. The original headliner is still in the car. I'm happy that I had a little something to do with getting this famous Mercury finally restored. But the best part was the day I could jump in it with McNiel and go for a cruise.

Another excellent clone/resto combination is the Barris-built Rev. Ernst '51 Chevy. In this case, the restoration came first. Burns Berryman of Rochester Hills, Michigan, once rode in the car as a kid. He finally found it again in Detroit in 1966, where some

And some builders simply clone their old cars. This is Bill Hines' recent redo of his *Lil Bat* finned '50 Ford, mounted on a late GM chassis for cross-country cruising.

contractor was using it for daily transportation and hauling shovels and sacks of cement in it. He wouldn't sell. Berryman continued to bid on it for 14 years, as it sat in a dirt-floor garage, rusting away. He finally got what was left of it in 1980, and with the help of four parts cars and metalman Jack Florence, he completely restored the car to its first Barris form over a 10-year period, debuting it at the 1990 KKOA Spectacular. Monsignor Ernst was present, and gave Berryman the working clock trophy the car won as *Hop Up*'s Custom of the Year in 1952.

Keith Ashley, owner of Fairlane Company in Michigan, makers of '36 Ford fiberglass bodies and other parts, also saw the Rev. Ernst custom when he

was in high school. It was the first custom he ever saw, and he never forgot it. He knew Burns Berryman and watched the tedious restoration of the original car. But the Ernst car was updated a couple of times by the Barrises, ultimately in a flamboyant lime green/bronze/gold three-tone version with inverted Cadillac taillights, rounded hood corners, and Pontiac bumpers. Harry Bradley, who patterned his *La Jolla* Chevy loosely on the Ernst car, has called this version the beginning of the end of tasteful, traditional, organic customizing. So Ashley contacted Bradley and asked him to, as Bradley put it, "tidy up the original car's rambunctious and rather hastily done design changes." This involved

things like fitting the bumpers closer to the body, shortening the overrides, extending the skirts and lower rear fenders, lowering the Continental kit, and refining the grille teeth. The physical work was started by John Kouw in Holland, Michigan, and finished by Randy Church Restorations in St. Charles, Michigan. Just like the overrestored Hirohata Merc today, this car is absolutely stunning, with a fit and finish—not to mention a flow of components—far exceeding anything that came out of the Barris shop in the early 1950s . . . or most any other custom shop of the time.

It is absolutely amazing how many original early customs are being found and restored today. Of "The Original Radical Custom Mercs" listed in Chapter 2, we know the Bettencourt-Zupan car was stolen from Dean Jeffries' parking lot around 1970 and has never been seen since. We know where the Sam Barris car is in New Jersey (very slowly being restored). We don't know about the Quesnel, Sonzogni, or Bugarin cars. But all the rest—Wally Welch's, Ralph Testa's, Bob Hirohata's, Fred Rowe's, and Buddy Alcorn's—are now beautifully restored. It probably costs more these days to clone a radical custom than it would to restore an original, if it's in anywhere near decent shape. But let's hope that both practices continue well into the future.

There were so many customs being cloned or restored at the turn of the twentieth century, we've barely covered the subject. This is the original *Marquis* '56 Ford that Cushenbery sectioned and highly customized for Gene Boucher in 1962. Bud Millard completed its restoration in 2000.

CHAPTER
TEN

When it comes to custom categories, I'd call this '50 Buick just plain gorgeous. It is obviously built in the sloper style, by Greg and Diane Davis in their own Davis' Body Shop in Hiawatha, Kansas. Finished in 2000, it is sectioned 3 inches and channeled 2-1/2 inches over a '77 DeVille floorpan. The top is a narrowed '68 Impala, the trunk is handmade, and the hood is pie-cut. And that's just the beginning of the modifications list. Greg said his intention was to build a car that "looked something like" the Sam Barris Buick. I think Sam would be right proud of this one.

156

THE NEW CUSTOM ERA: SLOPERS

THIS MAY BE THE

last chapter in this book, but it is by no means the last chapter in the history of the American custom car. The original plan was to end this study with the rebirth of customs, pegged to the first KKOA Leadsled Spectacular in 1981. At first glance it appeared there really hadn't been any appreciable growth beyond the 1950s-era, 1950s/1960s vintage cars, other than the occasional "billet and tweed" high tech custom (but still based primarily on 1950s vintage cars, like chopped '49–'51 Mercs). But, on second look, there have been several developments recently, so I've added this chapter to examine the state of customizing as of the turn of the century.

It begins with *CadZZilla*, the '48 Cadillac Sedanette designed by Larry Erickson and built by Boyd Coddington (with metalman Craig Naff) for guitarist Billy Gibbons of ZZ Top in 1989. I included it in the *Rod & Custom* All-Time Top 20 Rods and Customs, and I think it holds up to that. The emphases here are the term "designed" and the radically sloped hardtop roofline. Early customs may have been sketched on a napkin in a coffee shop by the likes of George Barris, or maybe even inspired by a "Sketchpad" by Tom Daniel or some other artist in one of the car mags (though I can't think of an example of one of these leading to the building of an actual car). More customs simply took shape as the cutting, welding, and fitting of components progressed. Neil Emory of Valley Custom once told me that the parking lot for one of the big aircraft companies was either behind or across the street from their shop in Burbank, California, and they'd wander through it periodically looking at headlights, taillights, grilles, side trim, or other components of newer cars that might be incorporated in customs they were working on.

But in the 1980s and 1990s, both street rod and custom car builders started relying more and more on design drawings for their car projects. I think it started with "graphics" designs, and it actually applied more to paint schemes for race cars before the rodders and customizers got into it. Guys like Ed Newton, Tom Daniel, and even Hot Wheels designer/rodder Larry Wood were designing "rods" during

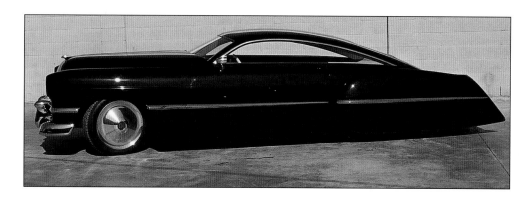

There's no question that the style of the latest custom trend was set by *CadZZilla*, the slope-roofed '48 Cadillac sedanette designed by Larry Erickson, built by the Coddington shops in 1989, and owned by Billy Gibbons of ZZ Top.

Another pair of excellent slope roof slicers are the Autens, Dave Sr. and Jr., who first rolled out a very slick candy brandywine '55 Merc in 1990, and then this slippery purple Buick in 1993.

The really fun thing about customizing today—just like hot rodding—is that you can pick any era you want. Jimmie Vaughan helped Mike Young of Austin, Texas, restyle his '60 Chevy Impala the way it would have been done in the early to mid-1960s. Gary Howard did the metalwork and glittery white paint; veteran Vernon McKean did the pearl white tuck-and-roll; and Rod Powell sprayed and striped the lavender accents. Recently, Young added an adjustable air bag suspension.

the zany show-mobile era, when fearless constructors would build the wildest things these artists drew on paper. But during the more realistic street rod and revived custom car era, the pioneer designers have been Thom Taylor, Steve Stanford, and to a lesser degree (volume-wise), Harry Bentley Bradley, followed more recently by Erickson and Chip Foose. With the exception of Stanford, who's just downright naturally talented (not to say the others aren't), these are all schooled designers, most products of (and in a couple cases teachers at) Art Center College of Design in Pasadena.

If you're going to build a 1950s-style custom from a 1950s car, you've got a pretty good idea of what you want and what it's going to look like, even if you're paying someone else to do the work. But if you're going to spend tens—if not

hundreds—of thousands of dollars for a fabricator to build one of today's swoopy, highly reworked, slope-roofed customs, it only stands to reason that you should start with design sketches, so you and the builder are on the same page. It's a lot easier to erase and redraw designs than it is to change sheet metal. Plus magazines such as *Rod & Custom*, *Street Rodder*, and *Custom Rodder* have continued to run numerous "sketchpad" or design theme pages, often by the above-named artists, and a surprising number of these drawings have been turned into real cars by enterprising owners and builders. A good example is Billy Gibbons' *Kopperhed* three-window '50 Ford custom built by Pete Chapouris' shop from a Steve Stanford drawing that appeared in *Rod & Custom*.

Other notable "slopers" would include Dave Auten Jr.'s black cherry '55 Mercury from Michigan in 1991, and even more striking deep maroon '50 Buick in 1993. Coddington's next one, also debuted in 1993, was the *Chezoom* '57 Chevy for Mr. Gasket, but I personally see this as a swoopy, overchopped top stuck on a shoebox. In 1994 a notable sloper was Angelo Fiorini's all-purple '50 Buick fastback from Florida, customized by John McNally, a top-chopper from that state who has gotten far too little credit for the work he has done. The next year upholsterer Kent Kozera of Visalia, California, rolled out *Kadzera*, which was basically a lowered and dechromed '59 Cadillac with a severely chopped and sloped roof. More recently, the summer of 2000 saw the intro of Greg and Diane Davis' gorgeous amber pearl '50 Buick fastback from Kansas. Built in the owner's body shop, he designed it as a modern version of the Sam Barris Buick.

Probably the most notable custom activity of the 1990s was (and still is) the voluminous productivity of Richard Zocchi and John D'Agostino to start with, followed by Rick Dore, and to a lesser extent Jimmie Vaughan and the late Manuel Arteche. Zocchi, of course, has been large on the custom car scene since 1962, when he had Gene Winfield very tastefully rework a brand-new Pontiac Grand Prix, first painted in lime green fades over Metalflake, then repainted tangerine pearl. D'Agostino, who is younger, but like Zocchi from the East Bay area of Northern California, arrived on the scene with a purple chopped '51 Merc that I featured in the June 1986 issue of *Hot Rod*, and which was named to that year's *HRM* Top 10 list. But it was in the

It's surprising what a large percentage of the current custom world is locked into 1950s styles. But a daring few, such as customizer Jim Farcello of Carson City, Nevada, realize that they can do whatever they want while customizing a car—hopefully with eye-pleasing results. His '57 Buick uses a late-model windshield for the sloper effect, rolls on large-diameter wheels seen through slotted skirts, and is painted a bright hue of candy tangerine (a very popular custom color in the 2000s).

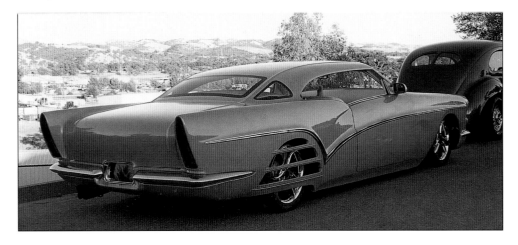

While they're more like project managers than builders, high-end customizers such as Zocchi, D'Agostino, and now Rick Dore have been turning out one, and sometimes two, new radical customs every year. How do they do it? In some cases by preselling them before work begins. That's what Dore did with this chopped and highly customized—and extremely rare—'56 Continental Mark II for Don and Flo Makofske of Allentown, Pennsylvania, that copped first in radical custom class at the 2000 Oakland show.

1990s that these guys began debuting new customs each year, usually side-by-side, at the Oakland Roadster Show and then again at the Sacramento Autorama. It has been a friendly rivalry. Many of the cars came from Bill Reasoner's Nor-Cal shop at first, and later from John Aiello at various shops. The emphasis has definitely been on chopped tops. D'Agostino was probably the first to favor big, long, low, and luscious luxury cars like Lincolns, Cads, Rivieras, and four-place T-Birds. John's first was a '56 Lincoln in purple

candy fades by Winfield that won the Harry Bradley Design Achievement award at the 1991 KKOA Leadsled Spectacular.

But this new/old custom frenzy really got going at the 1993 Oakland show, where D'Agostino had a candy red '57 Cad Eldorado by Jim Farcello with a Bill Hines paint job, Zocchi had a pearl white and butterscotch fogged (by Winfield) chopped '57 Dodge with Packard taillights, Rick Dore presented a very chopped '57 Buick fogged in pink, plus *Chezoom*. Jimmie Vaughan's lime green 1960s-style '63 Riviera also appeared that year, but not at Oakland. In 1995, D'Agostino had an Aiello-built, Winfield-painted (green fades) '57 Lincoln Premiere with a very sloped roof, done from a Thom Taylor design drawing in the December 1993 *R&C*. And the list goes on from there, including a '56 Continental MK II from Zocchi in 1997, and both a Stanford-

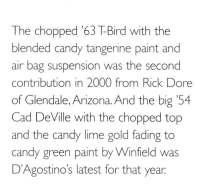

The chopped '63 T-Bird with the blended candy tangerine paint and air bag suspension was the second contribution in 2000 from Rick Dore of Glendale, Arizona. And the big '54 Cad DeVille with the chopped top and the candy lime gold fading to candy green paint by Winfield was D'Agostino's latest for that year.

While it does have a curved modern windshield, Andy and Diane Vendzuh's '49 Merc convertible isn't a sloper, but it is an excellent example of a high-tech custom. Built by Dave Auten Jr. in 2000, it is chopped a slight 2 inches and sectioned 3, with 17-inch billet front wheels, a blue top with gray leather inside, and painted bumpers and grille.

designed '57 Chrysler Imperial and a very chopped '61 T-Bird from D'Agostino that year.

One thing I'll interject here that's strictly my own observation is that way too much emphasis is being put on top chopping these days, especially by this highly competitive car show crowd; it's also probable that many of these tops are being chopped way too much. These newer, lower, longer, wider cars of the late 1950s and 1960s don't need chopped tops like the fat, bulky bodies of the 1940s and earlier 1950s. One pertinent example is the recently restored Larry Watson '58 T-Bird, which of course is unchopped. Why go to all the work and expense to chop the top on a car like this a couple of inches, when it looks just as good stock?

Some other 1990s trends: For the first time we have full-on fiberglass reproduction chopped '49–'51 Mercs, from both P&J Automotive in Virginia and from Gene Winfield. P&J also offers a complete repro frame and suspension to mount its body on, while Winfield's fits on an Olds station wagon chassis. Winfield also makes a fiber-

glass chopped '41–'48 Ford coupe in the Jesse Lopez style.

Thom Taylor single-handedly led the storm for bullet-nosed Studebakers, predominantly with his design for *Frankenstude*, which took nearly a decade to build. Shown at the 1992 SEMA show in bare metal, it was finished by builder Greg Fleury in 1998. Thom also propelled the popularity of slammed, molded, and big-wheeled giant Chevy late-model station wagons—about the only example of contemporary cars being mildly customized. On the other hand, it seems as if every hot rodder these days has a slammed late-model GM pickup with billet wheels, rolled pans, and possibly scallops or other custom paint. Why do all these people mildly customize new pickups, but not new cars?

What about cars like Troy Trepanier's '50 Buick fastback of 1992, or the more recent *Sniper* '54 Plymouth coupe and *Intruder* '57 Ford wagon, both for avid rodder George Poteet? They have lots of body modifications, but they also have hot engines and big billet wheels. I see them more as

What's this car doing in this chapter? Other than its bright pearl color, it's strictly traditional. Built from his own molds and painted by Gene Winfield, this chopped '47 Ford is all fiberglass. He can fix you up with a '50 Mercury, too, or parts thereof.

hot rods than customs, but once again the line blurs. The same thing could be said of contemporary "smoothie" street rods, especially '37 Fords and fat-fender Chevys. Most of these "rods" have as many body mods as the 1940s-era customs. I think it's mostly a question of which end of the car sits where . . . but you decide. I like rods and customs equally, so it's a moot point for me. I'll say one thing for the *Sniper*—it's one of the few rods or customs of the 1990s to tastefully incorporate one of the many shapes of new halogen headlights. Although it's fortunately not too prevalent, the turn of the century may be known as the era of goofy headlights, most cases being worse than the square headlights of the 1970s.

Finally, while we've lost a few along the line—Sam Barris and Clayton Jensen a while back, and Joe Wilhelm and Bill Cushenbery more recently—several of the original customizers are busier than ever today: Bill Hines, Dick Dean, Gene Winfield, Sam Foose, Bill Reasoner. A few are retired, such as the Alexander Brothers, Neil Emory, and Larry Watson. Some build special project cars, either for themselves or customers, on a limited basis: Joe Bailon, Frank DeRosa, Dean Jeffries, Dick Jackson, and newer-comers like Paul Bragg, Gary Howard, John Harvey, Merlin Berg, and Donn Lowe. The Bistagne Brothers and Dick Bertolucci parlayed their early custom shops into huge, thriving body shops years ago. And while each turns out a custom now and then, both Darryl Starbird and George Barris have been into promoting for the last few decades— either car shows, or cars for shows or movies. Of course this is a very partial list of the many people who contributed to customizing across the country over all the years. And, also of course, there continue to be dozens, if not hundreds, of owners and

As is apparent from this lineup of members of the Deacons club from San Diego, customs are a major part of the rod/custom mix in the many new 1950s-oriented clubs springing up from coast to coast. They're obviously not afraid to chop tops.

builders turning out traditional 1940s, 1950s, and 1960s style customs, which still remain the bulk of the hobby as it thrives today.

However, the really good news is that there's a new generation of customizers and custom owners developing. The several new, young, "retro" car clubs that sprouted in the 1990s, such as the Shifters, Deacons, Road Zombies, and Lucky Devils, plus a whole bunch of new ones on the East Coast whose names I don't know, mix early style customs with the rods, much as clubs did in the 1940s and 1950s. One Southern California club, the Choppers, which includes Jerry Weesner's son, Keith, and Robert Williams' nephew, Aaron Kahan, boasts several carefully researched late-1940s and very early 1950s full customs, painted in semigloss metallics. Most were constructed by young San Fernando Valley customizer Scott Guildner, who has turned out

several show-winning, early style customs lately. Even my own son, Bill, drives a slammed, wide-whitewalled '50 Ford mild custom with Olds flipper wheel covers and purple scallops. I don't know if you'd call this the second generation of customs enthusiasts and customizers—more like the third or fourth. But I don't see this trend dying out—again—any time soon. Long live the custom car!

The Choppers club from the Burbank, California, area has some very nice '40s-style customs, most with metalwork by Scott Guildner and metallic basecoat paint without clearcoat for a nonporous suede (matte) finish. This lineup includes Deron Wright's '41, Verne Hammond's '40, Keith Weesner's '50 Ford, and Sandy Wachs' F-100.

A CUSTOM CAR GLOSSARY

Air bags: A decades-old suspension system (used largely on big trucks) that replaces a coil spring or augments a leaf spring, using the compressibility of air inside a cylindrical rubber "bag" as the springing device. At the turn of the twenty-first century, they have become suddenly very popular with rodders and customizers as an adjustable suspension system. With small electric air compressor(s) added, along with air storage tank(s), the car can be dropped to the ground at the flick of a switch (releasing air pressure in the "bags"), and then raised back up relatively quickly by releasing compressed air from the storage tanks into the bags and refilling the tanks with the compressors.

Beater: A custom or rod that is unfinished (perhaps permanently), probably in primer paint, but driven regularly. Also, a custom or rod that was finished at some point but has since deteriorated from much use.

Bellflower tips: A type of chromed tailpipe popularized by customizers in the Long Beach, Lakewood, Bellflower area, such as the Renegades in the 1960s and the Sultans more recently, which exits behind the rear wheel, runs along the bottom of the rear fender, and terminates in a large pencil tip.

Beltline: The line around the body that separates the top, or roof, from the rest of the body. It is located at the bottom of the glass (or "greenhouse"), and often has a chrome strip around it.

Billet: Used as a noun or adjective to describe parts that have been machined or otherwise cut from a solid piece (or billet) of aluminum; not cast or welded. A billet wheel has a billet center attached to a formed aluminum rim.

Billet look: A street rod style highly popular in the 1980s, with all chrome and any other protuberances (e.g., hinges, handles) cleaned off the body; billet wheels; and numerous components (dash panel, taillight housings, mirrors, license frames, and possibly the grille) made from brush-finished aluminum. Some recent customs are built in this style.

Bondo: A common brand of plastic body filler, often used as a generic term. Use of too much Bondo, rather than good metalworking, to make body changes or fill rusty or dented areas is highly frowned upon.

Bondo barge: A car that has been customized or repaired with too much plastic filler; akin to the earlier "lead sled."

B-pillar: The vertical pillar between the two side windows of a sedan, sometimes called the doorpost. The pillars at the windshield are A-pillars, and the back of the roof is sometimes referred to as the C-pillar, but not often. A closed car with no B-pillar is a hardtop.

Bubble skirts: Long, often bulbous fender skirts that sometimes cover nearly the entire rear quarter of the rear fenders. Sometimes known as Turnpike Cruisers, for the type used on '57–'58 Mercurys, though usually handmade. As opposed to teardrop skirts or flush skirts.

Candy, candy apple: A transparent paint, tinted in any Kool-Aid color, that is applied over a reflective base coat (usually gold or silver) to produce a deep, rich hue.

Carson top: A nonfolding, padded, usually chopped, lift-off convertible top as made by Glenn or Bob Hauser at the Carson Top Shop in Los Angeles. Other upholstery shops, notably Gaylord in Lynwood and Hall in Oakland, made Carson-style tops, as well.

Channeled: Has the body lowered over the frame by cutting out the floor and rewelding it higher in the body.

Chopped: Having the roof lowered by cutting and rewelding the pillars, as well as cutting the glass. A chopped convertible has a cut and lowered windshield, and either a lowered folding top (very difficult), or a custom-made padded, removable, nonfolding top (e.g., Carson).

Color sand: Using very fine grades of sandpaper (e.g. 600-, 1,000-, or 2,000-grit), with water, to smooth the final coat of paint, before rubbing it out to make it look like glass.

Coupe: A closed, two-door car with a short roof and one seat. A '50s coupe might have two seats, but always a shorter roof than a sedan.

Fade, fadeaway: A paint job that blends one color or shade into another without a masked-off line. "Fadeaway" also refers to front fenders on '39-'48 Ford, Merc, or Chevy customs that have been extended to the rear fenders, giving a streamlined fender line like that on similar vintage Buicks. Also used to describe '49–'51 Mercurys with the "hump" taken out of the door.

Fastback: Certain 1942–1952 models of GM two-door coupes or "sedanettes" that have a roofline that slopes gracefully from the roof, through the trunk, without any "hump" at the beltline. This would include Chevy Fleetlines, similar Oldses and Pontiacs (with essentially the same bodies as Chevys), Buick "Supers," and Model 61/62 Cads from '47–'49.

Fat fender: A car with round, bulging, removable fenders front and rear; specifically '35-'48 Fords and Mercs and '36-'48 Chevys.

Fiesta: A three-bar flipper wheelcover used specifically on '56 Oldsmobiles of the same name, and more loosely on '54-'56 Oldses.

Filled: Generally refers to any part of a car body that has been welded shut and then smoothed with filler—for example where a handle or an ornament has been removed, or where seams, such as fender-to-body, have been closed.

Flames, flamed: A paint scheme of stylized, usually undulating flames that cover the nose, hood, and/or sides of a car. No rodder or racer would really want his engine on fire, but flames imply a truly hot car and give a menacing look. There are those who say a traditional custom should never be flamed, but painters such as Watson and Jeffries truly made an artform of it on the later 1950s cars.

Flathead: Any valve-in-block, or L-head, engine, but specifically the '32-'53 Ford and Mercury V-8.

Flipper: A wheelcover with one, three, or four raised bars that reflect light as the wheel turns; also known as a "spinner."

French: To mold the headlight or taillight housings to the body and install the lenses from the back side, often in a recessed manner. The term derives from the appearance of French cuffs. Also applies to any recessed component (e.g., an antenna) or one with a raised lip around it (e.g., an exhaust pipe).

Gloss coat: The final coat of paint that is sprayed on smooth and glossy, and which usually gets rubbed out on a custom; opposed to a base coat.

Hardtop: A closed car, primarily of the 1950s, with no door post or B-pillar. There were both two-door and four-door hardtops.

High tech: Contemporary custom styling featuring smooth bodies, minimal or painted-out chrome, brush-finished or machined bare metal (i.e., billet aluminum), and usually billet wheels with blackwall tires.

Hub cap: A small, decorative, usually chrome cap that covers the hub and the lug nuts in the center of the wheel. Not to be confused with a wheelcover, which covers the whole wheel. Rodders prefer hub caps; customizers prefer wheelcovers. The term "flipper hub cap" is a misnomer.

Hydraulics, hydraulic lifts, hydros: A type of custom adjustable suspension employing battery-powered hydraulic fluid pump(s), usually in the trunk, operating hydraulic lift cylinders between the frame and cut-down springs at the wheels, by means of switches in the interior. Hydraulics can be added to the front wheels, rear wheels, or both, and the switches can be set up to operate each wheel separately, or in pairs, allowing the car to dance front-to-back, side-to-side, or any number of combinations. Used primarily on lowriders, but have been adapted to rods and customs as well.

Kemp: In the 1950s a slang (specifically beatnik) term for a car in general. Today it has been appropriated by certain adherents to mean a custom car, or Kustom Kemp (as in the Kustom Kemps of America—KKOA—association for custom cars).

Kustom: In the early 1950s, for some unknown reason, George Barris always spelled custom, as well as other "c" words, with a K. His shop was Kustom City; he promoted a loosely knit club called Kustoms of America; and one of his custom trucks was the *Kopper Kart*.

Lakes pipe, laker: Originally a header with a cap (also known as a "lakes plug" or "cutout") that could be removed quickly for racing at the dry lakes without removing the mufflers. Today, a long, chromed, decorative pipe, with a cap at the end, that is mounted along the bottom edge of the body on a custom; also called a "kickstand" because of its shape.

Leaded, leaded-in: Before plastic filler (see Bondo), molten lead was used to fill, smooth, or recontour body areas. Anywhere holes were filled or seams were molded, the body was described as "leaded-in."

Lead sled, sled: Originally a derogatory term for customs in general (as used primarily by hot rodders), but especially for one on which body modifications were made by paddling on lots of lead rather than reshaping the sheet metal (see metalworking).

Lowboy: a name for a channeled, fenderless hot rod, as opposed to highboy, on which the body sits on top of the frame in the stock position (no matter how much the car is lowered by other means). This term does not apply to customs.

Lower: to drop the body closer to the ground, usually by cutting or flattening the springs or by reworking the suspension.

Lowrider: A car culture that grew out of customizing in the mid-to-late 1950s, centered in the Chicano community, which rapidly developed its own look, styles, and accessories (notably hydraulic lifts in the 1960s and straight-laced wire wheels in the 1980s). While a lowrider might be considered a custom car in the broadest sense, it is not a "custom" as discussed in this book. A custom is certainly not a lowrider.

Metalflake, flake: A kind of custom paint job consisting of candy paint sprayed over tiny aluminum foil squares, like glitter, usually silver, but in other colors, too.

Metalworking: Forming pieces of sheet metal into desired new shapes when customizing a car, rather than forming the new shape with filler such as lead or Bondo. The metal can either be formed off the car with a hammer and shot bag, English wheel, planishing hammer, or other metalworking tools, and then welded into the car's body; or the car's original body metal can be reshaped by cutting, reforming with hammers and dollies, and rewelding, often with the addition of new metal as well. "Metal finishing" refers to doing this process so well that no filler, of any kind, is needed.

Mild custom: a car that has been customized moderately (nosed, decked, frenched, lowered, etc.). A "radical custom" is one that has been chopped, channeled, or sectioned.

Nosed: Having the hood ornament and any chrome emblems removed from the hood, with the holes welded and filled.

Pearl, pearlescent: A custom paint said to have been originally made from ground fish scales (this may or may not be true). It is now made from mica particles. Mixed into, or applied over, any color of paint, it makes the color shimmer like the iridescent surface of a pearl or abalone shell.

Pencil tips: A type of chromed, straight exhaust tips favored by customizers, which have a swedged, or "rolled in" end; contrasted to belled tips, which flare out at the end more favored by hot rodders.

Pinstripes, stripes, striping: Thin lines hand-painted with a special brush ("dagger," "sword") with a short handle and long, tapered bristles on top of the body color, either accenting body lines, outlining flames or scallops, or creating abstract designs on the hood, trunk, or other areas. Although pinstripes go back at least to the days of Roman chariots, as well as furniture, carriages, bicycles, sewing machines, and so on, it was the late Von Dutch (Kenneth Howard) of Los Angeles who developed the intricate, fleur-de-lis pinstripe designs around 1955 that might hint at animals, faces, female figures, whatever. Other early rod and custom stripers include Tommy the Greek in Oakland, and Dean Jeffries and Larry Watson in the Los Angeles area.

Pipes: Exhaust pipes, especially the chrome portion at the rear of the car. It also refers to the fact that any rod or custom must have dual pipes, or "duals."

Radical custom: see "mild custom."

Rake: The stance of a car with the front end lowered more than the rear. Also known as a "dago," from "dago" dropped axles made in San Diego, California. The rake is partially caused by the fact that a hot rod has much bigger tires in the back than in the front. (This is also known as "rubber rake.") Traditionally, customs have the same size tires all around, and sit level, or with the back slightly lower than the front. Surprisingly, there is no term for this common stance, other than the slightly derogatory "tail dragger."

Roadster: An open (no solid roof) two-passenger car with a removable windshield, and no roll-up side windows. They were the cheapest and lightest model in the line, yet sporty—and thus the favorite of hot rodders. However, many people think "roadster" applies to any hot rod, which is not at all true, and the term would never be used to describe a custom.

Rub out: The final step in a custom paint job, in which the color-sanded paint is "rubbed" or "buffed" with a slightly abrasive "rubbing compound," either by hand ("hand rubbed") or with a rotary buffing pad, until it is very glossy. This is usually followed by a second buffing with a "sealing compound" or "sealer," and then hand waxed.

Scallops: A paint design of long, usually thin, tapered spears, either flowing backward from the nose of the car, or intertwined throughout the body panels.

Sectioned: A very intricate custom operation in which a section of the body is cut out, between the beltline and the bottom, and the two halves are welded back together, making the body thinner.

Sedan: A closed two- or four-door car with a long roof and front and rear seats.

Semi custom: A car show term or class that denotes a mild custom taken to the next level with substantial headlight/taillight changes, bumper changes, scoops, and so on; but not chopped, channeled, or sectioned.

Shave: To remove any chrome or other protruding parts, such as door handles. A nosed and decked car has been shaved.

Skirts: Removable metal covers that attach to the rear fenders, hiding the wheel and tire, favored by custom owners. Certain factory accessory types, such as the '40s Buick or Packard "teardrops" and the '57 Mercury Turnpike Cruisers were popular, as were handmade varieties, such as the long, bulging "bubble skirts."

Slammed: Severely lowered, especially in front.

Sombrero: A fairly recent nickname given to the large '49–'52 Cadillac wheelcovers, shaped much like a Mexican hat, that were standard on most early '50s customs.

Spinner: See "flipper."

Spot, spotlight, Appleton: A bullet-shaped spotlight mounted through the windshield pillar, just above the hood, generally of the Appleton brand. A "dummy spot" is a much cheaper substitute that has no inside handle or working light.

Stock: Unmodified; as built by the factory or original equipment manufacturer (OEM); not customized. Also known as "gennie," short for "genuine." This can refer to entire cars, or to component parts.

Street rod: Originally, a hot rod built primarily to drive on the street, as opposed to one built for racing. Since the late 1960s and early 1970s, it has been defined by the National Street Rod Association (NSRA) as a pre-1949 street-driven hot rod.

Teardrop skirts, teardrops: A rear fender skirt, obviously teardrop shaped, that fits over the wheel opening and has a convex shape; they came on factory '39–'41 Buicks, and some '40s Packards, as an accessory. They were fitted, almost uniformly, to the fat-fendered '36–'48 customs—leading, naturally, to their manufacture by custom accessory houses, such as Eastern Auto. "Teardrops" also refers to a singular pinstripe style, popularized by Tommy the Greek, consisting of long, thin, pointed shapes (like exclamation points without the dot), with one color in the center and a contrasting outline, usually in sets of three or five, side-by-side.

Tubbed: Describes a vehicle that has had the rear frame and rear axle narrowed, the wheelwells cut out, and larger wheelwell "tubs" installed to allow superwide "Pro Street" rear wheels and tires to be installed. This drag race–flavored style would seem incongruous on a custom, but a surprising number were built this way, especially '49–'51 Mercs and Fords, during the height of the "Pro Street" craze of the 1980s.

Tuck-and-roll: A type of upholstery, usually in Naugahyde (a brand of leather-look vinyl material), with rows of narrow, stuffed pleats in vertical or horizontal patterns (or both), popular in rods and customs.

Wide whites: Tall, skinny tires with 4- to 5-inch wide whitewalls, used in the 1930s through early 1950s. Medium whitewalls (also often referred to as "wide whites"), used in the latter 1950s to very early 1960s, have 3-inch white bands. Narrow whitewalls, used in the mid-1960s and up, have 1-inch bands in the middle of the sidewall. One style of these very popular with customizers in the later 1960s were U.S. Royal Masters, or just "Royal Masters." The 5-inch 1930s-style whitewalls are now often called "gangster whitewalls," especially by lowriders.

INDEX